Foot

The Apprentice
Season 5 Finalists

Back: Tarek Saab, Jose 'Pepi' Diaz, Andrea Lake, Bryce Gahagan, Lee Bienstock, Michael Laungani, Sean Yazbeck
Middle: Stacy Schneider, Leslie Bourgeois, Brent Buckman, Lenny Veltman, Summer Zervos, Dan Brody, Theresa Boutross
Front: Charmaine Hunt, Allie Jablon, Roxanne Wilson, Tammy Trenta

Roxanne Wilson

Footprints in the Boardroom

Roxanne Wilson
with
Kathryn Miller

THE APPRENTICE

SkyAiser
PUBLISHING SERVICES
Chandler, Arizona

Roxanne Wilson

All scripture quotations, unless otherwise indicated, are taken from the HOLY BIBLE, NEW INTERNATIONAL VERSION®. NIV®. Copyright © 1973, 1978, 1984 by International Bible Society. Used by permission of Zondervan. All rights reserved.

FOOTPRINTS IN THE BOARDROOM

Copyright © 2006 by Roxanne T. L. Wilson

Library of Congress Cataloging-In-Publication Data

Wilson, Roxanne, T. L.
Footprints in the Boardroom / Roxanne T. L. Wilson. – 1st ed.
p. cm

Library of Congress Control Number: 2006940542

10 DIGIT ISBN 0-9772099-1-1
13 DIGIT ISBN 978-0-9772099-1-0

1. Prayers
2. Communicating with God
3. Inspiration
4. Faith
5. Peace
6. Spiritual
7. Reflections
8. Devotion
9. Reality Shows
10. *The Apprentice*

All rights reserved. No portion of this book may be reproduced in any form without the written permission of the Publisher.

Cover Design by Bosgraphdesign

Printed in the United Status of the America

Chandler, Arizona 85249
www.skraiberpublishing.com

2006940542

Footprints in the Boardroom

Dedication

❦

This book is dedicated to my family whose continuous love and support give me strength and stability.

❦

Roxanne Wilson

Footprints in the Boardroom

Acknowledgements

To my sisters:
Rhonda, you inspire and challenge me to reach the bar you continue to set daily.
Rochelle, you are my conscience, my cheerleader, and my reminder to continue on when I am weak.
And Arian, you remind me to laugh, smile, and delight in life.

To my parents, Jeffrey and Patricia: Dad you are the one person on this earth who is arguably most like me . . . the Daddy's girl. I could thank you for so much, but most of all, I thank you for teaching me from day one that I am your child second, and God's child first. Mom, you are my heart. Every gracious part of me is an imitation of you.

To my fellow Apprentice candidates: Thank you for challenging me and traveling with me along this journey . . . our journey. The time we had will bond us forever.

To Donald Trump and Mark Burnett: Thank you for the opportunity to experience *The Apprentice*, and become a member of *The Apprentice* family.

To Mark Burnett Productions:
Production: Thank you for all of your hard work and care from step one through the end—you are the Heart behind *The Apprentice.*
James Sterling: Thank you for supporting me in my pursuit to share my story.

To Daniel: Thank you for your unfettered support and encouragement. You truly are my brother.

To Fred Miller: Thank you for your support from day one. Who knew that a phone call would lead me to where I am today? I am grateful for your counsel and support.

Roxanne Wilson

To Kathy Miller: Thank you for taking this stroll with me . . . reliving my experiences to retell a story. I have enjoyed every element of the process and thank God for you daily.

⁂

Contents

Introduction 1
Chapter one 5
Chapter two 11
Chapter three 17
Chapter four 25
Chapter five 29
Chapter six 43
Chapter seven 53
Chapter eight 61
Chapter nine 69
Chapter ten 77
Chapter eleven 81
Chapter twelve 87
Chapter thirteen 97
Chapter fourteen 105
Chapter fifteen 117
Chapter sixteen 123
Chapter seventeen 131
Chapter eighteen 135
Quotation sources 143
Biography 149

Roxanne Wilson

Introduction

"Every wish is like a prayer – with God."
~Elizabeth Barrett Browning

For as long as I can remember I've said my prayers. From a child kneeling by my bed, next to my father I prayed "Now I lay me down to sleep ...," to the quick "Help me pass this final Lord." To asking that God's will, always be done in my life. So it was not unusual to ask God to be with me on the journey that took me to the television show *The Apprentice*. And it was as natural as breathing when I got on the show, to go out on the balcony of the Suite and say my prayers.

My faith is very important to me and has guided me through every segment of my life. I have always felt the Father's presence beside me, always challenging, always reassuring, with me always. With Him as my companion and guide all things are truly possible. I look for His Footprints in every challenge; this is how I know that no matter how difficult the road may be He will direct my path. When I first entered the boardroom of *The Apprentice* His footprints were already there. So as I began the journey that would lead me from being asked to help find contestants for *The Apprentice* to actually competing, and then making it to the Final Four; I took with me the knowledge that prayers had sustained me through tough times in college, law school, and while establishing my career, and they would continue to be a part of my daily routine.

I prayed as I always do. When I get up and when I go to bed, and in between. I prayed before each task, during the tasks, and after the final results were in. Prayer is second nature to me, there were times when I needed to be alone, to have God all to myself and feel like I could truly focus. That is when I would go out on the terrace at the Trump Suite where I lived with all the other contestants during the production of *The Apprentice*. There I would look out at the lights of the city, all the way to the river and the busy streets below, and talk to God. I asked for guidance. I offered thanksgiving. I petitioned for forgiveness and I praised His Name as best as I know how.

Journaling has always been a way for me to have conversations with God. Most entries simply melt into prayers which I read over and over again. My prayers and the prayers of family and friends were my support throughout the amazing journey of being on *The Apprentice*.

My book is more than just an account of the prayers I prayed leading up to being chosen for the show, and during the times on the balcony and in the boardroom. It is my journal turned into conversations with God, becoming a fervent prayer. It is my affirmation of the goodness of God, the love and support of family and friends, and the remarkable everyday surprises of faith. My gratitude for the entire experience and what I learned along the way continues to give me strength, and courage to pursue the next leg of the journey God has in store for me.

Lord, my prayer is that you will give me the strength and courage to make it through each test I encounter. I pray this is the beginning of something new, something challenging,

something awesome in my life; something I can learn while living in – but not of – the world. I have dreams, Lord; I pray they are your dreams as well. No, I pray that they are Your reality. I remember that 'I can do all things through Christ who strengthens me.' Let that be my prayer, O Lord, and my comfort. Amen

ം‌ം

> "Prayer is the key of the morning and the bolt of the evening."
> ~Mohandas Gandhi

Roxanne Wilson

Chapter One

So, here I am, Lord, sitting on a plane getting ready to go to Los Angeles for the finals. I guess I'd better recap all that has happened leading up to this time.

In late June, 2005 I received a message from the Baylor Alumni Association. They had received a call from the reality television show *The Apprentice*. The producers were coming to Austin to audition for potential contestants and wanted Baylor University grads. I was excited! What a great opportunity! After several days, I finally connected with *The Apprentice* people and got all the information and the flyers to disperse. At first I didn't think about seriously applying, but my friend Jennie emailed me constantly and earnestly encouraged me to submit my name. I must admit that I had begun to think about it; but there were always those self doubts and false hindrances that kept cropping up. Soon after, another friend, Michelle, called and said I should try out. I think after both of them gave me their unsolicited thumbs up, I was 100% (absolutely) ready to go.

Very soon after that, I attended a Baylor University alumni dinner. During lively dinner conversation I mentioned the auditions for *The Apprentice*. Fred Miller, a Baylor alum and film producer, seriously encouraged me to pursue this opportunity. While at Baylor, I had been in the Baylor documentary "A Most Significant Journey," and Fred knew my work. "Great copy" he called me. To be encouraged by Fred was the green light to go ahead. So I got busy. I pushed Baylor to send out the announcement to the alumni, and I dealt with the doubters and skeptics who asked, "Are you sure this is not fake?" I told them over and over, "No, this is for real."

By Thursday, the day of the special audition for local university grads, I was ready. I made an appointment with my hair stylist Mechelle, so my hair would look great. As fate would have it, the previous week, Mechelle had just moved to the Omni Hotel. The auditions were at the Omni! How cool was that? So my hair looked fantastic. I felt good and I appeared casual, and not at all nervous.

The night before I spent four hours typing my application. Little did I know, that would be the shortest of the applications to follow. There were people auditioning from Texas Tech and Texas State University as well as Baylor. The casting crew came out, gave us the "skinny," told us the interview would last about ten minutes, and gave us the order in which we would be called.

When my turn came I said a quick prayer and walked in.

Please forgive me of my sins and let me do my best, Lord. Your will be done in there. Thank you, Lord.

The audition went well. I met the casting directors Toby and Kara. I had been in contact with Toby while dispersing the information to Baylor grads. The session was fairly relaxed. One of the questions on the application was to write about an ordeal we had encountered in the workplace and describe how we overcame it. Kara and Toby wanted me to elaborate on the answer

Footprints in the Boardroom

I had given. So we talked for a while about that and other things. Time flew by and eventually Kara said they loved talking with me, but had to keep moving. When I went back out into the hall, an alum from Texas Tech said "You set a record. You were in there twice as long as anyone else." I didn't realize how long I had been in the audition. Another applicant said, "We will see you on *The Apprentice*." I just smiled, wished everybody good luck and left. *I hoped, no prayed, Lord, that what they said would be true.*

When I did not hear from the producers the next day I was very disappointed. But then I realized there were two more days of casting. *Roxanne, Hello!* I kept myself busy as best I could with work and activities. Whenever I thought about it I just said a quick prayer for patience; which is something I possess very little of. I remember turning on the local morning news station and seeing *The Apprentice* applicants standing in line outside of the Omni hotel. As the news reporter was interviewing Kara, the casting producer I met just a day ago. I listened intently hoping to get a clue as to how it was going or how I matched up. The television told me nothing. I did not tell many people I had tried out because I didn't want them to laugh at me or doubt my ability to make it. So I spent the entire weekend stressing alone about what could happen.

On Sunday, I got the call. I was cleaning. I never clean. I paced around my kitchen with my cleaning rag in one hand as Toby told me that they wanted me to return for an in-depth interview. This time as I walked into the Omni, I WAS nervous. I sat waiting my turn for what felt like forever. I tried to slow my breathing and keep my thoughts positive: "Just go in there and be your fabulous Roxanne," I told myself (whatever that meant). I couldn't stay calm. When my turn came, I prayed, and peace came. I made it through the interview. However, I did sweat a lot. On my back! And I don't sweat on my back. I hoped they couldn't tell.

Next they wanted me to make a video. "So this is where you get your act together, Roxanne." I said to myself as I bought a camcorder to start taping my life. That evening we were at a party for my church young professionals group and a friend took the

7

camera and announced she would shoot video of me. "This is great!" I thought, as I rushed home excited to look at the footage.

I eagerly turned on the video and was shocked when I saw what I had. My big debut was mere shadows and a salt shaker! Twelve minutes of a salt shaker! And the rest was all dark! That was when I realized I was going to have to step it up a bit.

The next morning I woke up and asked myself if I really wanted this. I realized I did, but I had to do things right. I used my resources. *God, you are so good.* That is when I called Fred Miller, my friend the film producer. He told me what to do. "Call Daniel." So I called Daniel, a cinematographer, and he began taping. The next thing I know, I have scenes laid out, a camera man and a video with a really good ending. It was stressful, but it all came together. Daniel was awesome. He took off a week of work, went to a 6 a.m. Jazzercise class, and followed me around. When the video was shot, it was hard to choose a cut so quickly, but the video was finished and I loved it. I sent it away and prayed for the best.

More waiting. Soon I got another call and more paperwork. By now I believed I might have a chance. Then a couple of days later I got a package that would lead to a call and a flight time to LA. I was in the final 50!

Wow, Thank you, Lord. Here I am, sitting on the plane for Los Angeles. So much had to happen in such a short time, but I am at peace with it. I pray you watch over me and help me to remember to be myself. Help me to take this all the way. Lord, I keep hearing from my friends that I ought to be on the show and it makes me nervous. Because it's one thing to hear it from your friends and another to hear it from the "experts", those who do this for a living. And I'm wise enough to know to get on the show is just the beginning of so much. Am I afraid of that? I want to embrace the challenge in front of me if I am cast on the show. I realize it might be scary, but I really do want to do it. I just need to BELIEVE in myself. I pray for the courage to be who I am and show them Roxanne; to walk in there and be unafraid to put myself out there. I thank you millions of times over, Lord, for bringing me this far and I pray that I please you in everything I do. Amen.

> "Prayer does not change God, but it changes him who prays."
> ~Soren Kierkegaard

Roxanne Wilson

Chapter Two

❦

"Prayer is the confession of one's unworthiness and weakness."
~ Mohandas Gandhi

The week in Los Angeles was a whirlwind of activity. Before the final interview I knew what I needed to do, but I was not feeling as confident as I wanted.

Lord, I just need to go in there and be honest. I can do that. I have more peace about that today than I did yesterday. Lord, give me the tools that I need. Let me see this interview as an opportunity and not a scary, frightening experience. It is not only a job interview, it is a personality interview. Lord, give me strength. Please, Lord. Amen.

Roxanne Wilson

I've often thought about a process in terms of "baby steps", sometimes referring to myself as the "Baby Steps Girl." But today was a "Big Steps" day. "Big Steps, Rox." I prayed that I would knock their socks off. I thanked God for getting me this far. But when I left, I was so unsure. No amount of telling myself how much bigger than life I was, or how I deserved to be one of the finalists would calm me after the interview. My doubts came crashing down. It sapped me of my confidence. Waiting for the outcome was agony.

Dear Lord, the final interview is over. I mulled over the experience for the rest of the night, wondering how I could let this opportunity slip through the cracks. How could I come this close and fall apart? I now know that I am the "baby steps girl." I know what I have to do to win this whole caboodle. Another hurdle must be climbed. I do feel like the lack of confidence can be a help – not a hindrance. A lot of soul-searching is required. That basically means I need to ask You to tell me who I am and that I need faith -- faith that You wouldn't have brought me this far without a reason. Thank You, God, for your guidance.

I'm going to New York! I'm on *The Apprentice*! I called my Daddy. I told him everything. He said he didn't know if he was shocked or surprised and that it would all hit him later. He asked lots of questions like: "Where are you? How long have you been there?" I told him and then he said, "Well, I really don't know what *The Apprentice* is because I have never seen the show." But he was familiar with Donald Trump and the phrase, "You're fired." So I briefly explained the premise of the show. Donald Trump gathers 18 people, mostly young professionals, to compete in numerous tasks involving everything from renovating a Boys and Girls Club to running a huge fundraiser to designing a promotion plan for a national product. The contestants are divided into two teams and the team that loses has to face Donald Trump and his assistants in the boardroom. In the boardroom a contestant from the losing team is fired each week, and all the others continue to compete until there are only two left. In the season finale, Mr. Trump will hire one of the finalists to be his apprentice for a year. This would be the fifth season.

After I told my dad about the show, he had a few more questions before he enthusiastically congratulated me. Then I called my sister, Rochelle, to share the good news. They were SO excited!

I didn't sleep much and woke up very early on the morning I was to go back home. My friend Jennie called at 5 a.m. and I told her the great news. Then I went down for breakfast. NO one that I knew was there, so I did some writing.

A song came on while I was sitting there. It was "When I Fall in Love." It made me smile because it was my first solo, ever! I was in 7th grade choir. How funny and soothing and what a memory trigger.

Soon I was on the plane, headed back to Austin to tie up loose ends, and get ready for an exciting new adventure. **Two and a half weeks! There is so much to do. So I pray that God will tell me what to do.**

And, by the way, Lord, could you do it in two and a half weeks?

I'm back home now faced with the overwhelming magnitude of what I have to do yet I know I will get it all done. It reminded me of law school. There I was with tons of books, notes, treatises and I had no idea how I was going to make it until the end of the semester. But I did. So I can do this, Lord, with your help. Amen.

I felt God had opened a door for me and I had to go through it. I had to give up a lot of different things. Oh, I don't mean I had to sacrifice, but I had to give up my Jazzercise classes, my job at Winstead Sechrest and Minnick PC – complete my work and turn my clients over to others in the firm. My boss, Judge Craig T. Enoch was so supportive and coordinated my departure as a leave of absence. I had to find someone to take care of my puppy – Bear. But the hardest thing to do was to give up the young professionals group at my church which I had helped start. It was called *Untitled* and I was on the leadership team.

Roxanne Wilson

After I had been attending Riverbend Church for a while, some of us realized that the community offered nothing for young Christian professionals – college graduates, with no kids- who needed contact with other singles. It is a time in your life when you are by yourself. It was mind-boggling; to live in such a city, where there are so many of us, but there was not a group for us. So we founded *Untitled*. We started with six or seven, grew to fifteen by the first meeting and when I left for New York it was over a hundred strong. It was awesome and I felt like I owned the group. But just when you think you own something, God reminds you that he owns you. Just before I went to Los Angeles for finals I had to decide if I was going to wait and see whether I was chosen for the show or go ahead and resign from my position before our first leadership retreat. I had poured my heart and soul into the group. I realized that I had to back off. I knew what I needed to do. I felt at peace. Peace does come over me ever so often. Everything was clear. I knew that whether or not I made the show, it was time for me to take a step back from the leadership team. So by faith I gave it up.

I think sometimes God gives you the gifts you dream of or desire, but you have to be willing to give up another gift he gave you prior. You've got to leave everything to go on a journey and experience it to its fullest. It's all part of His plan. And so, as wonderful as *Untitled* was – it was my baby – I was ready to move on.

Dear Lord, it is the morning I am supposed to leave for New York. So much has happened and I am ready. And I'm excited and I thank you. It has been the longest three weeks of my life. Time has slowed down. Lord, I am stressed right now, but I know you will guide me, rid me of all my worries and fears. I pray that you will take care of me through this new and exciting adventure/experience/life-change. You are constant. Anchor me, dear Lord, and help me to be myself and care not what others might do or say. Because in the end You are all that matters. Thank you Lord, let the journey begin.

Footprints in the Boardroom

Now here I am Lord, on another plane, bound for New York. What a blessing this whole process has been. Frustrating, but a blessing. I'm committed to take this all the way. I am my worst critic and I need to figure things out. I need to shine. Faith in myself is what I need. Wow. It is real. I have had to say good bye, cut things off and step back from what I love to get to this point. Funny, how that works, though, the peace that you have given me really works. You never give me anything I can't handle, Lord, and you are always by my side, so as you sit next to me in Row 21, "Let's do it." Amen.

છે~જી

> "Do not be anxious about anything, but in everything, by prayer and petition, with thanksgiving, present your requests to God. And the peace of God, which transcends all understanding, will guard your hearts and your minds in Christ Jesus."
> ~Philippians 4:6-7

Roxanne Wilson

Chapter Three

"If the only prayer you ever say in your whole life is 'thank you' that would suffice."
~Meister Eckhart

I arrived in New York on a Thursday. I was so anxious to get there and finish the job. Wonder where I got that? "Finish the job." The year before the Baylor University Women's Basketball team won the national championship, they made it all the way to the Sweet Sixteen. The following year, Coach Mulky-Robinson told her team that they had to "go back and finish the job." They adopted "finish the job" as their slogan the entire year. And they did! They won the NCAA Women's Basketball championship! And even though I am just beginning, and the goal is an individual one, I want to make it to the end. That is my ambition. To make it to the finish line. To be the next Apprentice!

Roxanne Wilson

I feel that I am here for a reason, Lord, and that I have much to learn and a lot to give by being on The Apprentice. I pray that I will let go and let You direct the adventure.

The first meeting with Mr. Trump and all the other contestants was surreal. I had to keep reminding myself that I was really there, thinking: "This is real. This is starting. This is not trying to get on the show. Roxanne, you are really on *The Apprentice*."

We all arrived separately at Republic National Airport where we waited for Mr. Trump. No one said a word. I looked every candidate in the eye hoping to capture a glimpse of who they were inside. I could hardly believe that this was the beginning. George and Carolyn, two of the executives who worked with the Trump organization appeared and led us to the jet pad where Mr. Trump was waiting. After inviting us all in to his jet, and introducing himself, Mr. Trump introduced George and Carolyn and told us they would be assisting him in evaluating the tasks we would be performing. Then Mr. Trump asked us to introduce ourselves. And that was surprising, too, because everyone was throwing out their credentials left and right and it was quite something -- there were restaurant owners, millionaires, venture capitalists, high- tech managers, immigrants, some who had pulled themselves up from nothing—you name it. All were extremely qualified. And I was just trying to get a handle on it, trying to get a grip on the whole event while it was happening. I didn't want to miss a thing. I didn't want to forget a single moment.

After introductions, Mr. Trump picked two people, Tarek and Allie, to lead the first task and pick their teams: Gold Rush and Synergy. I had a flashback to my elementary school playground when I prayed to God that I wouldn't be the last one picked for the game. That prayer is the first prayer away from the bedtime or meals that I remember praying passionately. I knew that Tarek and Allie were choosing who they thought would be worthy to be on their teams. I wasn't picked last. **Thank you, God.** Allie chose me for her team which was the beginning of what would be a life-long friendship.

As soon as the teams were picked, we were given the task and it was "Bam, here is your first task. Go do it." We piled in the van and headed to Sam's Club to sell memberships. And it was business school all over again. You have people talking – just to show you how knowledgeable they are. Nine people trying to show they were influential on this task. So it was very interesting. And I just kept thinking: Am I really here? What does all of this mean? Do I belong here? Am I worthy? It took a while for my thoughts to get to: Yeah, all these people are qualified, but you are qualified, too. You belong here, Roxanne. Then I knew. I belonged and I intended to stay a long time. I breathed a prayer of thanksgiving as we approached our destination.

The task was fairly straightforward. The team who sold the most Sam's Club memberships won. Two team members would be in the blimp, circling overhead advertising the event. All the others would be selling. I really didn't want to be in the blimp; it's hard to be a part of a team if you are up in a blimp.

Don't get me wrong, it would be awesome to ride in a blimp. I remember going to Arizona State University games with my family and seeing the Goodyear blimp up above. At times that was the highlight of the game, so to be given the opportunity to ride in a blimp was tempting except my goal was to compete and not hover over Sam's Club in a blimp.

Thankfully, I was not assigned to blimp duty. Brent and Stacy had blimp duty. I would be on the floor selling memberships to strangers. I had never sold anything that way before – cold sell. I prayed that my natural skills and my experience with customer service as a Jazzercise franchisee would be ample preparation. After initial plans were designed and assignments given, Synergy— the name we picked for our team -- headed to the Trump Tower to explore the Suite.

The first time I walked into the Suite with my teammates – the newly formed Synergy – was a mixture of tentative emotions. Since we had already started our task, my mind wouldn't let me fully enjoy the Suite. But it still was exciting. It was an awesome palatial suite. The Victorian-designed space was huge! We walked through the famous wooden door and started exploring the rooms. All were spacious and elegant -- first the sitting room, dining room, and living room, all beautiful. There was the game room, the fitness area, with a basketball court and exercise equipment. The kitchen was fully equipped and had two huge tables where the eighteen of us ate most of our meals.

When we started traipsing through the bedrooms, it was like negotiating a maze. What caught my eye was the balcony just outside the bedrooms. You could see nearly to the river on one side, and up to Central Park, and then gaze on midtown all from that magnificent terrace. The sounds of New York City filled the air. The balcony would soon become my haven for prayer and for a needed reality check from time to time.

When I went to pick my room, I learned that the four other ladies, Allie, Tammy, Stacy, and Andrea, had paired up as roommates earlier in the day. I was so focused on the task I didn't think about roommates. This left me, four men, two rooms and a cot. Sean and Michael quickly paired up. The cot was a reminder that if we lost, in a few days, one of us would be gone. I thought about volunteering for the cot for a few minutes, but finally decided that I didn't want to get fired and never have slept in an actual bed in the Suite. So I picked a bed knowing I might have to share a room with one of my male team members. Pepi didn't want Brent to be stuck in the cot – and the blimp -- all on the first task, so he took the cot. I started life in the suite with Brent and a framed picture of his wife as roommates.

Though I was in awe of our terrific living quarters, I was so immersed in the task that I couldn't think much about it until much later. On the morning of the task, I started out okay. But after a while it got easier, because selling Sam's Club memberships wasn't too different from what I had done every Sunday with *Untitled*, where I greeted people and tried to make them feel comfortable. It was just talking to people and I loved doing that.

After each task, the losing team was brought into a large conference room called the "boardroom" to meet with Mr. Trump and two of his assistants. The project manager and other team members are given a chance to explain what happened in the task and offer suggestions about who should be fired. Mr. Trump and his assistants – sometimes George and Carolyn, sometimes Bill Rancic, the first apprentice, or Mr. Trump's children Ivanka, and Donald, Jr. who work for their father – would question the team members, offer observations and ultimately Mr. Trump fired one or more of the candidates. Most of the time, Mr. Trump would ask the project manager whom he or she would like to bring back to the boardroom with them, where "someone will be fired."

The task completed, we were directed to meet with Mr. Trump. When we were all gathered together to find out the results, my heart was beating fast. I wanted to have a win behind us. I wanted to stop holding my breath and just relax. I hadn't had the courage to unpack my bags and really move into the suite. I didn't want to unpack and then repack because we lost or even worse because I was fired. So for the entire week I lived out of my suitcase. Crazy, I know. All the others had unpacked their things as soon as they arrived, but I waited.

George and Carolyn reported to Mr. Trump and to us the results of the task. Our team won by three memberships! In that moment I released a little bit of the anxiety and gained a little bit of confidence. When we returned to the suite I felt free to unpack. As I began to put my things away I realized that I hadn't unpacked because of a lack of faith, but rather, because I just wasn't ready. It wasn't time. But now I could move into what I hoped would be my home until the finale of the show.

I was so excited that we had won, and of course I wanted to reach out to my family and friends, but I couldn't because of show confidentiality. I did talk to my sister and when she asked how I was, all I could say was "fine, now tell me about your life." Rochelle loved it because I had to listen to her without talking.

This was just the beginning of a frantic, exhilarating, unbelievable experience.

Thank you, God. I'm so grateful to be here and be in this position. Each day is so new and different. I want to prolong this experience as long as I can. I keep telling myself of all the opportunities, not only for myself, but for other people as well. I need to go back to baby steps and prayer, enjoy the moments, just be present, just be grateful to be here. Everything I have is because of you. You are giving me

Roxanne Wilson

strength, courage and confidence to help me follow your will. Thank you, Lord.

☙❧

"Faith and prayer are the vitamins of the soul: man cannot live in health without them." Mahalia Jackson

***The Apprentice* finalists introduce themselves at Republic National Airport, and the competition begins**

Roxanne Wilson

Chapter Four

಄಄

"Prayer is nothing else than being on terms of friendship with God."
~Saint Teresa

We won the first task by a few sales, but the second week our team crashed and burned. It was failure upon failure. It just stunk. Our task was to create a guerilla marketing campaign using text messages, for Gillette's new Fusion razor. The team with the most text messages wins that task. Pepi was the project manager. We ended up in bathrobes in the middle of *Times Square*. The entire task was utter chaos.

I'm usually the conservative one. I'm NEVER confident that we have this task in the bag, but to lose by as much as we did was horrible. The first person I look at when we lose is myself. I critiqued my actions and asked what I could have done better. I began to think that I might be in jeopardy of being fired. People say that is crazy, but to NOT think you might be fired when your team loses, is vain and would be missing the mark. It could be anyone.

Lord, sometimes I give myself such a hard time that I forget to believe in me; I forget that I can do it all because I am your child. I think everyone is so qualified that sometimes I forget that I am, too. Part of this process is a faith walk with you, Lord. I pray that you give me strength, courage and confidence.

I prayed a lot going in to the boardroom, because I knew that I would be going against the rest of the team which meant I was on my own; well, hardly on my own – God was there.

All of the team thought that one member, Brent, should be fired. Except me. I thought that Pepi, the project manager should be fired. To be on a team of nine people you just met, people who were well qualified, and be the lone wolf who said, "I just don't think this is right. I don't think we should be ganging up on this person. Yes, he is all the things you say he is and maybe more, but he is not the reason we lost." That is kind of scary, because you know that any one of those nine could "gun" for you. However, I just felt adamant about calling it the way I saw it. Some of the others tried to convince me otherwise, but it didn't change that pit in my stomach that told me I needed to speak up even if it was going against the grain.

I stood my ground because God gave me the strength and courage to call it the way I saw it, even though I knew I was taking a big risk. Surprisingly, I wasn't punished for stating my opinion.

I wasn't brought back to the boardroom after that loss but evidently Mr. Trump agreed that the issues on the team were not the result of something Brent had or had not done, but rather the fault of Pepi, the project manager. I didn't feel like "I told you so", but rather I felt happy that I wasn't afraid to lift my voice for what I believed was right. I felt supported and affirmed; I was buoyed by the results.

I *remained* a little nervous about how my team would react to the fact that I didn't go with the flow on the Brent issue. But that night was so crazy for everyone in the suite that it seemed to be the least of their concerns. The fact that we lost two of our team members, Pepi and Stacy, that Brent stayed, and that Andrea ran off crying was all surreal. It took a long time for the Suite to settle down.

But there were lessons learned. Thank you, Lord.

Going to the boardroom is about scrutinizing every little issue, every action, and every thought. The challenge was the point of the game. That was the main reason we were all there, but we were also there to learn. Whether we learned to speak up even against adversity or to be loyal to a teammate, *The Apprentice* is a learning lab all the time. Waiting in the Suite to see who would come back from the boardroom was hard. When Gold Rush's members were getting fired it was a little removed; but when it is one of your teammates, you realize that part of your team will be gone and the dynamics will change forever.

Thank you Lord. I find amazing comfort in my faith in you. I pray I make you proud. Please give me the keen eye and ability to shine.

I keep thinking of sports and competition. Thank you for teaching me that– with your help – I can sink the three-pointer at the buzzer. Give me the strength to run this race with endurance, looking to you as the author and finisher of my faith.

Lord, I know you have a plan. I must trust in you. Along the road will be bumps, there will be hurdles, but I feel your strength and your comfort. Amen.

Roxanne Wilson

> *"Do not pray for easy lives. Pray to be stronger men. Do not pray for task equal to your powers, pray for powers equal to your task."*
> *~Phillips Brooks*

Chapter Five

❦

"Prayer does not use up artificial energy, doesn't burn up any fossil fuel, doesn't pollute. Neither does song, neither does love, neither does the dance."
~Margaret Mead

After our team lost the second task and Pepi was fired, there was some tension on the team, but I was confident in my ability to speak up for what I felt was fair. In the end it is always Mr. Trump's decision. Mr. Trump agreed that Brent was not the cause of our loss. To be a part of the team, we had to forget our personal feelings about team members and concentrate on winning the tasks. If we wanted to win, we had to put prejudices and resentments aside and look for the strengths in each team member.

For the third task, each team had to design an outdoor corporate retreat for dealers and owners of General Motors, centered around the unveiling of the 2007 Chevy Tahoe. We had to plan all day activities, plus creative ways to promote the new Chevy Tahoe. The team that received the best evaluation from the executives would win the task.

Andrea was the project manager and she did a good job on that task facilitating our ideas about how to create a first class retreat for the owners. We all stepped up to do our part and as a result Synergy won. I was assigned the task of designing all of the signage as we like to call it. And when I say all, I mean ALL of it. I was in charge of ensuring that the branding ran seamlessly through our event. Every element of our event was an opportunity to remind the guests of the theme. For example the signs denoting the retreat activities such as fly fishing, golf, etc. and the lanyards worn by our guests, employees, and the models all contained our event branding. You would be surprised how many places and ways a brand can be subtly and directly incorporated. The signage looked great and the team was pleased. I was pleased with what I had accomplished.

The entire event was a hit. We had some "snafus," like the park prohibiting us from conducting skeet shooting inside the park, but we were able to adapt on the fly and the attendees had an awesome time. We also had a golf cart collision, but the Chevy executives laughed it off. During that task, I felt something growing inside of me – confidence that I really belonged on *The Apprentice*. I wasn't yet eager to take on project manager, because it didn't feel like it was time, but I could if no one else did. We had a clear and convincing victory which reaffirmed our ability to work as a team despite personality conflicts.

But what was so exciting, was that we put away our second win and headed for the sharks. That is, we swam with the sharks. It was a really remarkable reward. Mr. Trump arranged for our team to go to Atlantis Marine World on Long Island. When Mr. Trump announced that our reward was to swim with sharks I was shocked and scared. Typically the rewards are nice dinners, meetings with important people or something mainstream. Swimming with sharks is not mainstream. My first thought was:

Footprints in the Boardroom

"What about my hair?" My next thought was: "What if I die?" I quickly answered both questions. I could go get my hair done at a salon after my swim, and if I died, Mr. Trump would take good care of my family. At that point I was ready to take on the sharks.

We talked about the sharks all night long. Brent and Andrea were both tense about taking the plunge, but Allie, Michael, Sean, Tammy and I were ready to go. In fact one of Michael's dreams in life was to swim with sharks. How perfect. We got up early the next morning and headed to the Aquarium. The director of the Aquarium gave us a tour and showed us the sharks that we would be swimming with. This was the first time the Aquarium allowed any outsiders to swim with the sharks. After our tour we went to the dressing room and changed into wet suits. Getting a wetsuit on is an ordeal in itself. Allie, Tammy and I took a while getting the suits on, and then we headed up to the top of the tank. The tank was at least three stories deep. There was an observation area downstairs where the tank was literally from the floor to the ceiling. From the observation area you could see about ten feet below and ten feet above. If you took the stairs up, you ran into the top of the tank where we would enter and swim with the sharks.

We split into groups of two for shark swimming. Tammy and Michael went first, and then Allie and I followed. As I slid into the water, I was taken back to my eight years of competitive swimming in Arizona. We moved to Arizona when I was six; Rhonda, Rochelle and I immediately joined the swim team. First it was just a summer hobby, but when summer ended, our love for swimming was just getting started. With the help of our parents, we found a United States Swimming team (USS) and swam year round. My events were the breaststroke and the individual medley. Every weekend we would pack up the minivan and head north, south, or in the Phoenix area for a weekend swim meet. If I could tally the hours spent in or around a pool in my lifetime, the number would be outstanding. Some of my best childhood memories surround swimming. Swimming taught me discipline and the prayer. I used to pray as I would get on the starting block:

Roxanne Wilson

Please Lord, give me the strength to get in the water and make a personal best.

As I spent time in the pool during a race, I had no one to talk to but God. Talking to God kept me focused on the race and stopped my mind from wandering. As I came to an important turn or got tired and wasn't sure if I had the extra umph to make it, I would pray*:*

Lord, I think I have given it all I have. Please help me to find just a little more to finish this race with endurance. And remind me that I have all the time in the world to rest after I get out of this water!

And when I hit the wall and finished, as I waited in the water for the race to end, I would thank God for making it through regardless of the outcome. I also prayed hard and fast with anticipation when I cheered my sisters on in their competitions. With my nerves going, I would cheer as loud as I could and pray just as hard that my sisters would do their best. These memories put me at peace with the challenge I was about to face.

As the memories of swimming engulfed my head, I spent a few minutes in the shark tank getting acclimated to scuba breathing. Since I had never breathed with scuba gear, it seemed difficult at first, but as I became more comfortable with the breathing, I prayed that I would not get eaten by the sharks. When I was situated, Allie came into the tank. We watched the sharks and other creatures. There was an orange looking snake-like animal with a dinosaur-like head. As we were dancing underwater we could see Tammy and Michael outside the tank smiling at us.

After Allie and I got out, Brent and Sean went next. Brent was nervous, but he did it and we were all proud of him. He would have regretted not taking the plunge. Speaking of regret, Andrea was compelled to get into the tank as well. In the end, we did it as a team. Swimming with sharks brought our team closer together. Whenever you share a rare experience with others, it brings you closer. Thank the good Lord it ended in happiness and not tragedy.

Footprints in the Boardroom

Each day here is a unique experience. Watching Mr. Trump with Carolyn, George and Bill evaluate each team fairly in a business setting, yet with the always-present knowledge that the TV cameras were rolling was very valuable.

After the second win and swimming with the sharks, I was more eager than ever to keep up the pace and prove to myself that I belonged on *The Apprentice*. I continued my prayers of gratitude and tried to keep my conversations going with God.

Lord, I will go willingly as far as you wish. May I have the courage and confidence to take risks and glorify You.

Getting to know my teammates was a high priority but balancing the relationships with the intense schedule of going from task to task and the pressure that goes with that to win was challenging. To understand all of the people on the team meant listening and watching. At times I just didn't have the luxury of evaluating all the body language and conversational nuances – so I had to go on gut feeling, and God's guidance.

The fourth task we were given was the Grape Nuts Trail Mix Crunch ad campaign. We were to create a billboard that would promote the new Post Grape Nuts Trail Mix Crunch cereal. The Post executives would determine the winning billboard.

Sean, Allie, and I were sent out to find the models for the billboard. Instead of using professional models, we had to go to the streets of New York to locate models. That was so much fun, running around New York. When we selected the models we wanted, we took them to the studio, picked out the outfits, and talked to our other team members. We were really relaxed. By that time we were in the studio, directing the models, guiding them, telling them, "yeah, that looks great," or "try it this way," we felt very confident about our product.

The process had allowed me to get to know Sean and Allie much better. It's as though we could anticipate how the other ones wanted the ad to look. We completed the shoot and had worked so well together that Allie and I were just "slap happy." We started eating the cereal out of the bowls, with only our mouths, giggling, laughing, and just being ridiculous. It felt like family.

Roxanne Wilson

We lost the task, but the community I felt was so important, because we all worked so well together, without conflict, and we lost the battle together. Afterwards, Allie, Sean and I lamented the loss, but still felt good about the way the team had worked together.

In the boardroom, we supported Tammy as project manager and were in agreement about how the task was completed. When Mr. Trump asked me whether Tammy was a better project manager than Andrea, I gave my honest opinion, "Yes," and then explained why. Andrea was audibly and visibly bothered by that. Although I didn't have time to think about it then, I would soon learn the repercussions of "crossing Andrea." Because of Brent's outlandish behavior in the boardroom, Mr. Trump fired him.

I was reminded of an entry in my Purpose Driven Life journal, from a couple of years ago. From my journal, the title of the day's entry was "You Are Not an Accident." I had been discussing that same point with my sister, Arian, and thought, "Cool. I like knowing that we aren't accidents and that we each have a purpose." It makes each day more meaningful. I may not know why I wasn't given certain gifts or why I was given the gifts I have, but somewhere down the line, I think I will make some of the connections that come from the relationships I am forming while I'm on *The Apprentice*, getting to know Allie and Sean and Tammy and Andrea and all the others.

Dear Lord, I love knowing that you spent time and thought on my creation. Knowing that you spent time on me makes facing the future all worthwhile. I'm not an accident. This isn't luck. It is You.
Thank you. Amen

ಆೊಈ

"Pray for a tough hide and a tender heart.
~Ruth Graham

Footprints in the Boardroom

Gold Rush and synergy receive their Tahoe Corporate Retreat Task

Roxanne Wilson

Sean, Roxanne, and the 2007 Chevy Tahoe

Roxanne Wilson

Footprints in the Boardroom

Synergy tours the Aquarium before swimming with the sharks

Roxanne Wilson

Footprints in the Boardroom

Roxanne and Allie style Synergy's Post Cereal Model

Roxanne Wilson

Chapter Six

❦

"Certain thoughts are prayers. There are moments when, whatever be the attitude of the body, the soul is on the knees."
~Victor Hugo

After the first few weeks I settled into the routine and knew, finally, that I belonged on *The Apprentice*. I was eager to prove my leadership as a Project Manager. I had confidence that I was up to the task; confidence given to me by God. I knew that I could lead a team. As the first female president of the Baylor University Chamber of Commerce I honed my leadership skills as chair of the homecoming parade as well as the Diadeloso (Day of the Bear) - the spring holiday for students. I had to supervise teams, delegate responsibility, and manage people's fears. I knew how to deal with budgets, various personalities and details. I was ready.

My first task as Project Manager was to create a 30-second commercial promoting Norwegian Cruise Line's Freestyle Cruising. We boarded the cruise ship and met the executives. Oh, wow, was this going to take some fast thinking and producing.

The night before I had prayed:

Now Lord, I need to step it into high gear. I need to be reminded that this is a faith walk with you and I can do it. Remind me through your calming voice that with you, Lord, I can do all things. Please give me the strength, confidence, faith and hope to lead tomorrow and be the best that I can be. Help me realize that I am smart and capable. And yes, I pray that we will win the task and I will stay in the Suite.

One of the things that happened on this task was the realization that even though I was project manager, there were those on the team who could make it difficult for me to manage the project. Andrea tried to take over and do my job. Every step of the task was marred by Andrea's open disapproval of how I was performing, what the concept was, and my not doing things her way. I assured Andrea that we were progressing according to plan. I acknowledged her concerns and I did all this as graciously as I could even as I was stewing on the inside. Well, Andrea's negativity became infectious. Suddenly, half of my team was losing confidence all because of one "doubting Thomas." I felt deflated. While listening to my teammates concerns, I had always given my team the utmost respect when they were project managers, regardless of whether I agreed with their style of leadership or the concept of our project. At the same time I knew that I was leading this ship and had to maintain calm. Add to that the fact that I was the only African American candidate on the show and did not want to create an opportunity for another negative portrayal of African Americans. I kept asking God if this was really what He meant for me. Was I really going to go down in flames because I wasn't getting any support from half of my team?

Soon, no one but Allie agreed with the vision I had for the commercial; I felt so alone. Even though Allie was very supportive through the whole process, the others didn't think my idea would work. And worse, my team refused to go down the path of simply trying the concept without constant complaints every few minutes. The conflict continued until I couldn't take it any longer. God doesn't give you more than you can handle and I had reached the limit. I reminded my team that I had always given them the respect a project manager deserved and explained that I didn't always agree with their ideas, but I remained a team player. I only wanted to be treated the same way. I couldn't believe I had to stick up for myself. I was naïve in thinking that they would give me the same respect as I gave the team. Once I realized that I had to either stick up for myself or go home, my outlook changed, and things got better. I knew that my actions would either win the task or send me packing. Lo and behold, my strategy worked. After clearing the air, the teammates who were unsupportive kept quiet and the rest of us charged into gear. I decided to go it alone and stick with the original plan. It was a hard decision because I knew if we lost, the team would rally against me, but if I went along with the flow, I wouldn't believe in the product.

We all went home around 4 a.m. There were still a few hours of work to do before our presentation, so the next morning I took Sean with me back to the editing bay, and had Allie stay with the rest of the team so she could keep an eye on the others.

Going into the presentation I still felt like the team wasn't behind me. As I worked on my presentation, knowing that I could do a good job, but doubting that my team was supportive, I became very emotional. I wasn't crying but the tears were right there. Pacing back and forth on the balcony, praying and practicing, I felt like it was just God and me. Later on, Allie asked me if I was praying out there and I told her I was. I just wanted to throw in the towel, to start over. A very lonely time. I just knew that if we lost, I would be gone and the team would rally against me.

The commercial came together and the presentation went smoothly. A simple, but straight forward and clear message won over the executives, and we won! I was so excited!

As our reward we were taken to a secret vault at Brinks Security where a diamond expert from the Plucenick Group taught us about diamonds. Each of us was allowed to choose a loose diamond to keep. What a remarkable reward. As I looked at the diamonds, I realized that I was indeed fortunate to be participating in this experience. I wanted to learn everything I could and not miss anything.

What I discovered from the task, or was reminded of, was that strength comes from the courage to step up and make necessary demands. In a perfect world, everyone on my team would have handed me respect just because I was project manager. Team captain, president of the club, chair of the committee, I'd done all that. But when there are seven different personalities, some of whom were not team players, a leader must be clear about expectations. I was clear. I got the job done. I had learned a new lesson.

It was not that different from being the first female member of the Baylor Chamber of Commerce. At Baylor University, I was having the best experience of my life – but it was the hardest. I never set out to be the first woman in the club, but I was simply unafraid to walk through a door that was cracked open for me. I was invited to Chamber's rush events and in fine Roxanne form, I "showed up." By the end of Rush Week I learned that Chamber had the hardest pledge period on campus. Add to that the unknown issues involved in being the first and only female in a 78-year-old organization for men and it could be scary. Some will say that pledging is difficult. But hands down, being the first female-paving the road for others, and dealing with conflict as well as those who would like to see you fail, was harder than any pledge period. Pledging is about unifying the pledge class; and I definitely had that experience. But the hardships I faced only solidified my relationship with God. Chamber was a great training ground for *The Apprentice*.

Lord, I can only do one thing—thank you and give all the glory to you. Lord, you are amazing and awesome and I thank you. You won the task. You reminded me once again that prayer is powerful and that you will and can carry me through anything. The emotions I felt over the last two days were so great – so massive. Lord, I couldn't handle the pressure without you. Thank you for helping me care about a project so much that it hurts. Thank you for helping me hold back the tears. Thank you for the wave of emotions. You had me going through every possible emotion. What a whirlwind! Amen

"When we take one step toward God, he takes seven steps toward us."
~Indian Proverb

Roxanne Wilson

Footprints in the Boardroom

Tammy, Michael, & Roxanne in the war room working on the Norwegian Cruise Line commercial

Roxanne Wilson

Footprints in the Boardroom

Roxanne enjoying "her diamond crown" (Tiara from the Escada collection) after her hard victory as Project Manager

Roxanne Wilson

Footprints in the Boardroom

Chapter Seven

෴

"Don't pray when it rains if you don't pray when the sun shines."
~Satchel Paige.

After my first win as project manager, I was so grateful, I couldn't wait to get on to another task. Not only did I know that I belonged on *The Apprentice*, I was eager for the next challenge. I also felt a peace that regardless of how everything turned out, I had given it my all and was in it for the long haul.

The next challenge was a dream task. We were to write a jingle for Arby's new *Chicken Naturals*. Now that is right up my alley. How many times have I wanted to compose a song and sing it? Our team not only had to create a jingle that pleased the client, but put it to music and record it with a professional band.

Roxanne Wilson

When you design anything for a client, whether it is an ad campaign, a marketing plan, a fundraiser, or a jingle, you want to create enthusiasm. You want them to love it! First of all, we had to assess exactly what the Arby's executives wanted the customer to know about the new product – what the message should be. Then we had to create the jingle that positively conveyed that message.

So there I was in the elevator after meeting with the Arby's executive team, humming the tune that had been running through my head. During the meeting a melody just came to me, then the words, a hook; I had the basic beginnings of a jingle. This is fun! I sang it for Synergy and the team seemed enthused. When we got to the studio, we began adding lines and before we knew it we had a jingle. Now we just had to go to the studio and start mixing.

Sean and I spent hours at The Lodge --the recording studio -- laying the demo track, auditioning singers, choosing instruments and making harmonies with our sound engineers Eric and Drew. Although Sean was the project manager, I was given carte blanche to make decisions. Putting together the jingle was like playing with building blocks – adding instruments and voices together to make a masterpiece. It was so much fun and it was so seamless. There was a point when I actually laid down the sample track! I got to sing and create the guide vocals for the singers. I felt at home making music. As I was laying down the sample track I looked up to see Carolyn Kepcher, sitting in the studio. She had stopped by to observe at the same time I was singing. I could not believe I was singing for Carolyn. After we completed the demo and chose our singers it was time for dress rehearsal.

As we were waiting for everyone to arrive, we had an impromptu jam session with the band. Allie, Tammy and I started jamming. It went on for quite some time. We were playing the cymbals, the cow bells, dancing and singing. It was such a bonding moment. I love music so much that any chance to jam like that is so meaningful. Then Sean came in and began dancing with us. It definitely felt like home.

I recall when I was in AWANA, a church organization for children and teens. (AWANA stands for Approved Workmen Are Not Ashamed.) Growing up my sisters and I participated in many activities – religious, educational and social. I remember one time

Footprints in the Boardroom

when my sister and cousin were struggling with their task and trying diligently to learn the scriptures in our AWANA workbook but it just wasn't easy. So I started putting the words to tunes. I remember sitting at the piano making up tunes so that it would be easier to remember. And it worked. I even remember one of them. "For it is by grace you have been saved, through faith – and this not for yourselves, it is the gift of God - Not by works, so that no one can boast." *(Ephesians 2:8,9)*

I also use jingles in teaching Jazzercise. Often I teach an instrumental routine and add a rap about upcoming events or promotions, making it up as I go along. The students love it and we all have a great time, singing and laughing while exercising. All those experiences helped prepare me for the jingle-writing task.

We presented the jingle simultaneously to the executives and a studio audience. The audience instantly moved in time with our music and their applause at the end was so enthusiastic and gratifying. We were sure the audience liked our jingle best, but we waited to hear what the execs of Arby's would say. They loved it!

That was an incredible win because our team worked so well together for that task. It was amazing to go from hearing a "hook" in my head during our meeting with the Arby's executives, to seeing a professional band made up of the best in the business singing our jingle, while the crowd and Mr. Trump danced along. Too cool! After such a difficult experience the previous week with the cruise line commercial, I was so thankful for an opportunity to shine, relax, and be in my element. Even though there still were issues to deal with, winning again was a boost for Synergy.

Our reward for winning the Arby's task was to eat a dinner unlike any dinner I had ever eaten - A six-course meal at the Alain Ducasse restaurant in Central Park, featuring white truffles which cost an obscene amount of money per pound. It was truly an incredible experience. As amazing as it was, I get as much enjoyment, if not more, eating takeout from my hometown Chinese restaurant- China Way- with my parents and sisters; or, at Maudie's with my friends in Austin dining on queso and scoops of "guac." There is nothing like good food and great company!

55

Roxanne Wilson

Lord, what a dream task! Creating a jingle. To be able to spend a day in a recording studio with the best of the best and then to sing and jam with the multi-talented band is a dream come true. Thank you, Lord.

This whole opportunity has been heaven-sent. I have been fortunate to work with huge companies and do amazing things. I am living in an awesome suite and I have swum with sharks, had lunch with Mr. Trump, learned about and taken home a beautiful diamond. Amazing stuff. And regardless of how all of this turns out, I thank you, Lord. I give all the glory to You.

Being project manager on the previous task turned the tide for me, Lord. I am here to give it my all; I am no longer sitting back. Don't get me wrong, I was working hard before, but I am going for it now. The last two tasks have allowed me to build up my confidence and for that I thank you, Lord. I have two comforts: your grace and mercy and your ability to carry me to higher heights. Thank you, again, Lord. Amen.

"God can pick sense out of a confused prayer."
~Richard Sibbes

Footprints in the Boardroom

Tammy, Roxanne, & Andrea adding lyrics to the Arby's jingle

Roxanne Wilson

Footprints in the Boardroom

Synergy victory toast over a private meal at Alain Ducasse at the Essex House

Roxanne Wilson

Chapter Eight

☙❧

"Pray as if everything depended on God, and work as if everything depended upon man."
~Francis Cardinal Spellman

By the time I reached the halfway point of *The Apprentice*, I had journeyed through so many emotions. I had experienced community, loneliness, exultation, disappointment, support, lack of support. I also encountered a variety of learning opportunities. I felt like I was reaching my peak at the right time, but I always wanted to jump ahead to the end. I will eventually know the end of the story, but somehow walking through these experiences brings me closer to God. I need to remind myself to pause and experience everything.

Lord I thank you for bringing me to the half-way point in this process. I pray that you will take me even further, dear Lord. I just trust you will give me the strength to keep moving forward. Lord, you are my strength, my shield and my salvation. Confidence in you is what keeps me moving forward in this journey and it comes from you, Lord.

Both Synergy and Gold Rush had such a great time doing the jingles and we were all sort of "slap happy." We didn't have time to go out but we wanted to do something fun, so I decided to turn the suite into a club - "Club de Suite". I made signs and went around inviting everyone to Club de Suite. We all got dressed up. We had a dance-off. I was the club owner, so I organized the competition. We had a bartender (Michael), a bouncer (Michael) and a go-go dancer (Allie). It was ridiculous. I mean, here were these professionals – playing make believe. But we had a great time together and it deepened our sense of community. You are never too old to play make believe. Work hard and play hard.

There were other times in the suite when I was able to just sit around and talk with the others. Times when I could forget about competition and just live – just be and feel comfortable with where I was, and the people I was with. Those were the times when Allie and I did lots of talking, lots of bonding.

Working on our next task with the Boys and Girls Club was another rewarding task. The task itself was giving to someone else. We were to renovate a room for the kids in the Boys and Girls Club, in 24 hours. It was a hard task. Michael was project manager and he was not a decision maker; he was a pontificator. He wouldn't make decisions and we had to work non-stop. We didn't get any sleep. I restlessly napped on a kiddy chair for half an hour at about 6 a.m. Literally, we didn't go home; we worked through the night. It was very difficult. Conflicts began to surface. The team was frustrated with Michael and Andrea. We were so busy trying to beat the competition that we often forgot what the task was all about. But the true reward was seeing the kids' faces when they saw the room. For a while we forgot our petty differences and just focused on the kids. And while one team had to win, the kids at both Boys and Girls Clubs won, which was really great, because they gained a community room. Thank goodness we won the task, even though we probably shouldn't have. Winning and doing something for the Boys and Girls Club was further magnified by getting to meet Daeshira.

Daeshira is a Make-A-Wish Kid. She is a remarkable young girl who has cancer and has already faced so many hardships, with more to come. Her wish was to go on a shopping spree at Toys R Us and we had the honor of granting her wish. So we took Daeshira on a shopping spree with her parents and her sister. To see the looks on their faces and the happiness it brought them was priceless. And you think: Why am I here anyway? Why am I here competing for a job? Then you realize that God puts you here for a reason and it was good for us to put all the competition aside and focus – not on ourselves, because I think this whole process can be so selfish – but to focus on Daeshira. That was such an awesome experience: to grant Daeshira's wish. What is even more notable is that she wanted to buy things for her family and her friends – not just for herself. So we said: "No take one of everything in the store!" She was so precious, quite the young lady. I'm completely enamored with her.

I realized that I don't have to get up every morning worrying about much. But Daeshira does. She has so much to worry about and yet something such as going shopping which some would see as minor, made her day; no, her life. Daeshira's parents and her sister were also wonderful. They were so grateful; her mom kept saying: "Thank you, thank you so much." One of the best things in life is giving to others and I'm glad that as cut throat as *The Apprentice* was, we were able to pause, take a moment and give back. Because of my experience with Daeshira, I am now serving as Shopping Spree Ambassador of the Make-A-Wish Foundation of Central and South Texas.

Thank you, Lord for carrying me through another task. Sometimes I get discouraged, but you manage to keep pulling me forward. This process is becoming more and more

complicated by the moment and I need to keep my head on. I look to you for guidance. Amen

> "A simple grateful thought turned heavenwards is the most perfect prayer."
> ~G. E. Lessing.

Footprints in the Boardroom

Gold Rush and Synergy receive their Boys and Girls Club Renovations Task

Roxanne, Allie, & Sean "karaokeing" during the Boys and Girls Club activity room renovations

Roxanne Wilson

Footprints in the Boardroom

Tammy, Michael, Roxanne & Sean look on as Wish Kid Dashiera arrives at Toys-R-US for her shopping spree

Roxanne Wilson

Footprints in the Boardroom

Chapter Nine

☙❧

"Is any among you suffering? Let him pray. Is any cheerful? Let him sing praise."
James 5:13

The Boys and Girls Club task was so difficult in terms of our relationships, that I was concerned about our team. Michael opted to leave the team for personal reasons – he had personality conflicts with nearly everyone on the team following the last task. So he went to Gold Rush. Seeing Michael go created a mixed bag of feelings. Yes, there was conflict there, but if we lost the next task after winning three in a row, then the blow would sting.

Roxanne Wilson

When Mr. Trump announced that the task was to sell P'EatZZas, a new 7-11 sandwich, I was encouraged. As everyone knows, Sean, Allie and I were a sales force to be reckoned with.

The challenge was to show an increase in sales at two designated 7-11 stores. Synergy began by sampling the P'EatZZa, two slices of pizza with sandwich in between. Andrea requested that she be project manager and we got to work. Having Andrea as project manager after the conflict that she and I had made me uneasy. I knew she was not a fan of mine and that was okay, but it also reminded me that I was a target, especially with Michael jumping ship to Team Gold Rush. But I put it in God's hands and remembered that fear was not a path I was willing to go down. If I did the best I could then that is all I could ask for and I would thank God no matter the outcome.

Once the selling began we went at it full force. I even held a dog walker's dogs so that he could go in and purchase a P'EatZZa. Sanitation workers, nannies, students, neighbors, and workers on their lunch breaks were some of our customers who gathered that day. At one point we even had employees from the neighborhood pizza joint coming in to buy the 7-11 version of pizza.

Although Carolyn, Mr. Trump's assistant, was unimpressed by our giveaway – the hat that didn't really tie in with the P'EatZZa – we increased sales in spite of our giveaway. It wasn't easy to sell the pizza sandwich – eaten cold, with lettuce included – but we did it and enjoyed the experience while we were at it. It was awesome and all that hard work paid off because we won the task convincingly.

After winning our fourth task in a row, the reward was flying to Washington D.C. to meet with one of New York's senators, Senator Schumer. When we found out we were going to have breakfast with the Senator, I was excited. I hadn't been to DC for leisure since I was a child. There is something majestic about our Capital.

Senator Schumer is one of the best known senators in the country and it was such an honor to meet him. We arrived in DC by private jet and headed to the hotel where the Senator was waiting. As we introduced ourselves Senator Schumer realized that his daughter and Allie both spell their names the same

Footprints in the Boardroom

way. The Senator's face absolutely lit up with pride as he talked about his daughter.

We went into a beautiful suite where there was a table set for us. Before we sat down, Senator Schumer took us to the window and showed us the amazing view of the White House. Once we began breakfast we discussed our ambitions and aspirations. The Senator gave us a sage piece of advice that he called "The Monday Morning Test": If you wake up on Monday morning and are excited about going to your specific job, then you know you are in the right place. If you wake up on Monday dreading the work day ahead of you, then you need to make a change. As the Senator shared his "Monday Morning Test," my destiny was affirmed. It is just like God to put people or words into action that affirm what the Holy Spirit – or your gut - is telling you. What I heard loud and clear was that I needed to reevaluate my profession. Hearing Senator Schumer, an accomplished politician and family man, make such a strong statement about how he lives his life and say what I knew to be true was refreshing.

When breakfast ended, we thanked Senator Schumer and took a stroll to the White House. Sean, who is British, was soaking in the experience; I was also in my own time of reflection. I am the first person in my family born in the U.S.A. My mom was pregnant with me when we moved to the States. Had my parents not sought higher education- earning their PhDs, I would have been born in Trinidad and my life would have been completely different. Would I have had been on this *Apprentice* journey? Who knows? My parents' decision to move to America and become citizens is a constant reminder to me of the magnitude of that title, American. I appreciate my country that much more.

As I looked at the White House, I thought about how my younger sister Rochelle and I are the only members of our family who could be President of the United States. I still remember watching my dad study for his citizenship. It was funny for me, still a student, to watch my dad, the professor on the other side of a test. In fine Jeffrey form he enjoyed learning American history and found it intriguing. It reminded me of when he returned from a day of defensive driving, he quizzed us on all the traffic rules. Similarly, my dad quizzed my sisters and me on American history, and pointed out the interesting facts and statistics. It was odd watching my dad learn something that I already knew but it was also educational, understanding how important the whole experience was to him.

As we left the nation's capitol, I was again reminded of how many times doors are opened and we don't know why. In life's journey there are many lessons we learn, people we meet, and paths we travel.

God, thank you for being by my side in all my travels. Help me to never forget who I am or where I am going. Amen.

☙❧

"As we express our gratitude, we must never forget that the highest appreciation is not to utter words, but to live by them."
~John Fitzgerald Kennedy

Footprints in the Boardroom

Team Synergy listens to Senator Charles Schumer's "Monday morning test"

Roxanne Wilson

Footprints in the Boardroom

Roxanne, Allie, Tammy & Senator Schumer chat as they view the White House from the Hay-Adams Hotel

Roxanne Wilson

Footprints in the Boardroom

Chapter Ten

ಞಲ

"Prayer begins where human capacity ends."
~Marian Anderson

After four wins, our team was beginning to feel confident, yet there were issues that weren't being addressed. Because of the wins, there was no reason to go to the boardroom for someone to be fired. Some of the team members projected negativity, even tried to sabotage the tasks. Others rejected ideas by the project managers or tried to take over. Yet, conflicts and disagreements were covered up by wins. There you are living and working with these people knowing that the team isn't really working as a *team*. At the same time, we were all in competition for the job as Mr. Trump's apprentice. It was like the princess and the pea – you know the pea is way down there, not apparent to the naked eye because it is covered up by fluff – the wins, but it still is a pain in your back.

Even though I wanted the issues resolved, I wanted Synergy to keep winning. Our task was to create a commemorative Ellis Island Program sponsored by Ameriquest. The team that generates the most revenues from the program wins the task. The night before the Ellis Island task, I prayed:

> *Lord, I'm trying to fall asleep the night before a big task. I need to talk to you first. A "fivepeat" would be awesome. I'd be so relieved. Even more relieved than in the last task. Lord, you continue to show me goodness and mercy. I must admit I am a bit nervous about this task. For no matter what happens....* (and as I was falling asleep) *I just thank you, Love, Roxy.*

We lost the Ellis Island task. I really wanted that win because Allie was project manager. So to lose just stunk. But you have to look for the silver lining, even when it is not obvious.

So when it came time to go to the boardroom, I was excited. There were lots of things I wanted to say about one team member in particular- Andrea - because it needed to be said. And it had gotten to the point where it was unbearable and it was only going to get worse. She had done things, even when we won to sabotage the task. It was also nerve wracking too, because I agreed to go to the boardroom if Mr. Trump asked Allie to bring teammates back to the boardroom with her. It's a risk going in to the boardroom, even when you are supporting someone. You run the risk of being fired. And the project manager can't say, "I'm bringing so-and-so to the boardroom, and, by the way, don't fire him/her." But I wanted to clear the air and say my peace. It was totally worth it.

When I spoke my mind to Mr. Trump in the boardroom, he was surprised because he thought Andrea was such a super star. I said, "When you win four weeks in a row, you don't see all those things and it all gets covered up."

Mr. Trump stopped the discussion and asked me where I went to law school. I told him University of Michigan and he said,

"Roxanne, you know what I think?" I kind of gulped and thought, "Oh, my God, I'm going to be fired."

But he went on to say that Michigan should be proud of me and Mr. Trump said, "You are a very good speaker... I would like to have you represent me in court. You are very impressive."

Mr. Trump's comments were special because I didn't go into the boardroom expecting or hoping or wanting anything like that. I just went in there wanting to give my honest assessment. It was another gift from God and that gave me confidence which I really needed at that point to keep on going in the game – in the competition. Mr. Trump fired Andrea. I was so thankful that I spoke my mind in the boardroom and even more thankful that Mr. Trump listened, and Allie was staying.

Wow, Jesus. I just have to thank you. I was scared. Fearful, I'm ashamed to say. I didn't know what was going to happen tonight. I was so fearful for Allie. I had such mixed emotions because I was so excited about finally going to the board room and calling it out the way it should be. Thank you for giving me the strength to fight as hard as I did tonight. There was a risk, but I felt it was the right thing to do. You keep reminding me that with great risk comes great reward. The reward of having Allie return was such a treat. Thank you, Lord. I feel so fortunate to be here.

God speaks in the silence of the heart. Listening is the beginning of prayer.
~Mother Teresa

Roxanne Wilson

Footprints in the Boardroom

Chapter Eleven

☙❧

"Our prayers should be for blessings in general, for God knows best what is good for us."
Socrates

Throughout the experience of being on *The Apprentice*, I maintained that losing didn't have to be the worst thing that could happen. Or "winning isn't everything." And even though we lost the Ellis Island task, the fact that Allie was able to remain on the show was a huge plus.

What remained, though, were the scars. It seemed like every time we overcame the "big bad," we had the scars to show for it. For example, back when Brent turned on Tammy when we lost the Post Cereal task, the rest of us stood up for Tammy, hopefully creating team unity. But because I said that Tammy was a better project manager than Andrea, it created strife on the next task;

Andrea's feelings were hurt and she lashed out. Similarly, after the Ellis Island loss, most of the team rallied in the board room and Andrea was fired. But the scars from that boardroom were deep. The reason was mainly a result of Sean's flip-flopping. Sean told Allie he wanted her to stay prior to the board room and then told Mr. Trump in the boardroom that he thought Allie should be fired. I realized that Sean was playing a game I didn't want to play. I respected his right to play the game, but I didn't want to be a part of it. It is so ironic that I thought conflict would be mitigated with the departure of those whose strategy included sabotage, but as the numbers dwindled, the real personalities of those who stayed were revealed.

Allie was understandably hurt. I was cautious. I don't know how Tammy felt. But despite my personal feelings, I was able to focus on the task and the team. I chose to channel that disappointment towards winning the next task definitively, and making a statement that the four of us could dominate.

Regrouping for the next task gave our team a new energy. Our task was to manage the grand opening of a Hair Cuttery Salon. Tammy took on the job of project manager as we set up the store and made plans for the event.

We were responsible for advertising, pricing, and selling. We had control over everything BUT the hair – which was a good thing. For most of the task, Allie and I were together. Allie and I had awesome chemistry! Whether it was getting the word out to the masses, or running the store, we were on fire. The atmosphere at the Hair Cuttery was full of energy. We were selling hair product to customers who were waiting for a haircut and/or just passing by. I can't count the number of times Allie sold six products at a time off those shelves. We didn't know how the other team was doing, but by pushing the products, we felt that could put us over the top. Carolyn dropped by to see how we were doing and seemed impressed.

Ultimately we won the task because of the amount of product we sold. It felt great to know that all our energy paid off.

As usual, Allie and I were in our element, selling, promoting and keeping the surroundings very lively. By then we were feeling pretty good. We had already won seven of the first ten tasks. I don't want to think we were over confident, but all of us felt like we had already met many of our goals. My goal to continue on the show was becoming a reality and I went out on the balcony and said my prayers.

So, thank you Lord for carrying me through another task. I pray that you will continue with me in this journey.

Our reward was to write a song with Burt Bacharach at the original Steinway Piano Gallery. I was excited about this reward. I love music. I love Burt Bacharach who has written like every song on earth! That morning, I got online and printed off a 12-page list off all the songs by Burt Bacharach so that we were ready. I was singing the songs as I was going down the list. The second I got to the studio, I was totally enthralled with the Burt, listening to his experiences, and making the music.

Although I was excited about the reward and sharing it with my team, I wished my little sister was here to experience it first hand. My sisters and I have an equal love for music. I think we get it from our parents. But my little sister Rochelle and I have full phone "conversations" where we sing together and harmonize on the telephone. We are so in sync that we will spontaneously add the same harmony at the same time (and then act annoyed). Rochelle and I love to reenact the scene from *My Best Friend's Wedding* where the cast broke out into *Say A Little Prayer* at the dinner table – the song performed by Tina Turner and written by BURT BACHARCH! Rochelle and I would also used quote the part of *Austin Powers* when Austin said, "Ladies and Gentleman, Mr. Burt Bacharach," and then Burt started singing *What the World Needs Now*. So intuitively I knew that Rochelle would appreciate this experience just as much as I did.

Thank you, Lord. What an honor and a treat. Thank you for all of it. I don't know what is ahead, but I pray that I will stay focused and rely on you. Amen

Roxanne Wilson

> "But when you pray, go into your room, close the door and pray to your Father, who is unseen. Then your Father, who sees what is done in secret, will reward you."
> *Matthew 6:6*

Footprints in the Boardroom

Synergy making music with legendary Burt Bacharach

Roxanne Wilson

Chapter Twelve

☙❧

"Call on God, but row away from the rocks."
Indian Proverb

The time that our team came together as a real team when no one was looking out just for themselves, but all for one, was the Outback Steakhouse task. The task was to host a tailgate event featuring Outback Steakhouse food at the Rutgers homecoming football game. At first that seemed to be right down my alley. After all I had been the chair of the Baylor University Homecoming Parade, and that is no small task. I agreed to be project manager and was excited about the challenge; I really enjoyed the university atmosphere. But from the beginning nothing went right. Luck of the draw put us in the less populated of the two tailgating lots – bad location, location, location. We wanted Rutgers cheerleaders, but Gold Rush had contacted them first. Our flyers weren't ready in time and Tammy and I missed the pep rally. Everything seemed to be falling apart. But we didn't give up. We kept on adapting. As we were driving home the night before the game, I suggested we deliver the food to the tailgaters to make it easy for them to buy our food. At first we weren't sure our plan would work. But Allie made a large sale to the baseball players and we kept things moving. All three of us, never giving in, never believing we couldn't get the job done. We were so in sync. Because of the bad "location, location, location," Allie and I hauled food back and forth across the street to Gold Rush's lot and sold exclusively over there. Gold Rush never even saw us!

I actually experienced a feeling of loneliness after that task. It was somewhat confusing because what had been a very bonding task was also a challenging one. We were totally exhausted after that task. We had all worked so hard, I felt we were successful because, as George put it, we "hustled." Every time we were bombarded with adversity, we rallied. We never gave up. I remember going out on the balcony – before we knew whether or not we had won. I was tearful and praying. I knew if we lost, I would need to go home. Not because I wanted to go, but because my teammates, Allie and Tammy, had worked their butts off and then some – they had done everything I had asked and I couldn't pin point anything either of them had done that would be worth suggesting that either of them be fired. But I was project manager and if our team lost then I was the one who needed to go. So I was completely prepared to go to the boardroom and say, "Hey, it's me, not them." I was solely responsible and nobody could take the fall for a loss but me.

As it turned out, we won the Rutgers/Outback task. Allie, Tammy and I worked so hard and believed so much in one another we felt we really deserved that win. That is if you can deserve anything. The three of us were on such a high after the win. We felt like a real team and were pleased with our performance. As three of the final five, we were determined to keep the winning streak alive.

Our reward was to take the Trump helicopter to the Raphael Winery on the edge of Long Island where we spent the day making our own personal wine. The three of us traipsed through the vineyard picking grapes and eating them off the vine. Then we stomped the grapes. I Jazzercised in my bucket. Tammy and I jumped into Allie's bucket and we all danced around in the grapes. By the time we had turned the grapes into juice, our feet were numb and wine-colored. Our escort dipped a fresh glass into each of our buckets and offered it to us. I pondered for a moment and then drank my own foot juice!

After we washed up, we went into the cellar and mixed our own wine. I felt like a mad scientist. We toured the beautiful winery then had a wonderful lunch out on the balcony overlooking the vineyard. As we each drank glasses of Roxanne, Allie and Tammy wine, we toasted our success, friendship and hard work. That was such a blast! The rewards for winning a task were always great, but short lived; then it was back to competition.

Looking back, the times I felt most part of a team were when we met with adversity. That just seemed to trigger a determination to keep going. It's totally "faith-based", because if you go through life and don't have an understanding of a higher power, things might appear doomed. I always believe that there is something better out there and that something may be as immediate as five minutes from now or the next day or …. who knows? My Dad always says: "You know the darkest hour always comes before dawn." And I think that is so true; it has proven to be true over and over in my life.

Thank you, dear Lord, You continue to take me to new heights – more than I could even fathom. Amen.

"Arranging a bowl of flowers in the morning can give a sense of quiet in a crowded day – like writing a poem or saying a prayer."
~Anne Morrow Lindberg

Roxanne Wilson

Footprints in the Boardroom

Roxanne carting Outback Steak House food to Rutgers University Homecoming tailgaters

Roxanne Wilson

Footprints in the Boardroom

Roxanne, Allie, & Tammy arrive at Raphael Vineyards on Long Island, after being transported in the Trump Helicopter

Roxanne Wilson

Footprints in the Boardroom

Roxanne, Tammy and Allie stomp grapes to create their own labeled wine

Roxanne Wilson

Footprints in the Boardroom

Chapter Thirteen

☙❧

"Pray that you will never have to bear all that you are able to endure." Jewish Proverb

As we approached the eleventh week, Allie, Tammy and I were pretty jazzed that we had made it so far. We each had at least one win as project manager. Our confidence was high, but not out of bounds. Our task was to create an X-Box 360 display in Wal-Mart. Tammy was project manager on the Wal-Mart/Microsoft X-box project and we had troubles from the very beginning.

As Mr. Trump was introducing the remaining five candidates to the executives, he said, "Allie is from Harvard Business School, Roxanne is from the University of Michigan Law School, Lee is from Cornell, and Tammy...I don't know where the hell Tammy is from." When we got into our van, Tammy was visibly distressed by Mr. Trump's comment. Tammy said it was obvious that Mr. Trump didn't know her and that she wanted to make a statement by being the project manager. Her statement changed the entire dynamics of our terrific trio. During the task, there was not the typical sharing of ideas. I had ideas for our concept, but when I offered them it became clear that Tammy was on a one-woman mission. It was frustrating and disappointing to be silenced and although I worked hard on my tasks – which, by the way I was the only one assigned multiple tasks that had to be accomplished simultaneously – I had a bad feeling about the outcome. At one point Tammy, Allie and I sat down to discuss the tension. During that time, what I had been feeling nonverbally was finally verbalized: Tammy said that "this task was supposed to be <u>All about Me</u>." I was astonished. Despite that, I hoped we would win the task and march into the final four. Unfortunately, we lost.

Lord, give me the strength to articulate my words clearly, concisely and factually. If it is my time to go, Lord, I will go. But every fiber of my being is telling me it isn't my time to go. Am I crazy, Lord? My goal is to be the last woman standing. Only you know if that goal will become a reality. To be here is such a blessing.

After we lost that task I felt betrayed by some of the things Tammy said. Tammy blamed the loss of the entire task on me! I was totally disappointed to hear that as well as other negative things. I don't even want to rehash all of the things said in the board room. Bottom line: it just hurt.

Lord, as much as I am hurt by the betrayal, I am conscious of the need of support and comfort for those who tried to bring me down, and pray that she will find comfort in you. I was mad and hurt at the things that were said, but I still want to pray for her. She needs You, too, God. I always say: "Don't believe your own hype." And I truly believe that this boardroom was an opportunity to bring me down a few notches. And for that, Lord, I thank you. I pray that I

Footprints in the Boardroom

will work harder knowing what I heard in there tonight. Thank you for all you have done. I'm surprised, which is silly because you are able to do anything. Lord, forgive me and thank you for your patience with me. ☺

Please give me the courage to stand up for what I think is right. Amen.

❧❧

> Grace isn't a little prayer you chant before receiving a meal.
> It's a way to live.
> Jackie Windspear

Roxanne Wilson

Footprints in the Boardroom

The final five receive the Xbox/Walmart Task

101

Roxanne Wilson

Footprints in the Boardroom

Tammy and Roxanne in a heated boardroom

Roxanne Wilson

Footprints in the Boardroom

Chapter Fourteen

☙❧

"Our prayers should be for blessings in general, because God knows best what is good for us."
~Socrates.

The Apprentice experience was coming to an end and I had been through a myriad of experiences. The episode in the boardroom when Tammy was fired was so fresh in my mind and heart. I was so upset. Many of the things Tammy said about me, I didn't believe and didn't agree with, but the hurt was there. The things she said were not so important as the effect her words had on me. Instead of reveling in the fact that I was one of the final four, I couldn't stop rewinding the entire experience, trying to remember where and/or when she came up with the situations she mentioned. Accusing me of "riding Allie's coattails, bringing Allie down, that I wasn't serious." Those things shook me to the core.

I wanted to believe she was my friend, but then I realized: Come on, Roxanne, it's a competition. But unfortunately, I didn't always think about that.

As a celebration of still being on *The Apprentice,* it was usually the custom to do a toast when contestants came back to the suite. And we did that, but this time it was bittersweet. It was hard to celebrate a victory when so many negative things had come out of it. I just could not be happy about it. I even thought, "This is not so much fun anymore." But... I made it to the final four!

The next morning Allie and I had to get up and start on the next task. I wasn't ready. I wasn't feeling completely together. And when we showed up for the task, Mr. Trump referred to the night before, saying that we had been hard on Tammy, I was confused. Though I didn't say anything, I thought, "But you fired her, so you must have known it was the right thing to do." The wound was still there – an open, bleeding wound.

My confidence had been shaken to the core.

And yet, I had prayed about that very thing the night before. The funny thing about prayer is that even when I was praying for Tammy, I was mad. Mad and hurt. That didn't keep me from praying or giving thanks to God. Sometimes we don't know why things happen. Sometimes the disappointment is so real and confusing. And I'm impatient for answers. My dad's "darkest before dawn" reminder gives me hope to get through the rough times. But when the dawn doesn't come when I think it should or soon enough, I just have remember that *God's time* might not be *my time,* even though I want it NOW.

Lord, have I reached the end of the road? I don't know. It's only for You to know for sure. All I can say is: What an incredible journey. Thank you, Lord. Give me grace and help me overcome all the obstacles that are facing me now. Forgive me, Lord. I'm learning so much and it would not be possible without You.

Footprints in the Boardroom

Allie and I prepared to take on Lee and Sean. We were challenged to design new uniforms for some of the employees of Embassy Suites. Namely the chamber maids, cooks, bellmen, and front desk personnel. Allie and I took a long time to pick a project manager. How do you pick? I was 2-0 and she was 1-1, so it was okay to give her another chance to go up 2-1. I was fine with that, even though it would have been great to go 3-0; it wasn't that deep for me.

So Allie took the helm as project manager. I just wanted a pleasant task. Because of the tone of the last task, I went into our final one very cautiously; choosing my words and actions wisely. I didn't always agree with some of the artistic direction we were going. Just minor things – like should we put the women at the front desk in skirts or pants? I did voice those concerns; however looking back, I know I didn't voice them strongly enough. But my confidence had been so shaken on the last task, that I wasn't being "Roxanne."

I even tried to talk to Allie about how to speak to the designer because I felt her approach was not right, but again, I chose my words carefully, not wanting to cause unnecessary stress. Allie and I were both stressed out and I didn't want to lose again. I didn't want all those negative things that were said the night before to become a reality. I didn't want to give anyone fodder to be able to say, "Hey, I was right about Roxanne."

The actual task was interesting. I thought our uniforms were beautiful. They were risky. But you know when you go to a fashion show, all the clothes are edgy. They are not something you are going to wear. It's just a look. You figure out the other details, the practical stuff, in production. We designed skirts for the women at the front desk when they had said they wanted pants. Even though the skirts looked good, that was a mistake.

We knew we had lost when we went to the fashion show. Everything was beautiful, but when Lee and Sean came in, they were so cocky and full of themselves. We applauded for their uniforms, but they didn't for ours, they just smirked. Allie and I could tell from the reactions of the audience that it was not going well for us. During the actual show, Allie turned to me and said,

"This is not good," but I told her to be positive. "Stay positive," I said- always the constant cheerleader.

When the employees voted Sean and Lee's uniform designs as their choice, Allie and I were bummed. That meant one of us would be going home. And that was not what I had wanted. From the beginning I had wanted to be the last woman standing. Before the end of the last task, I wanted it to be Allie and me. All the way. So that was the *worst* day. I was so discouraged.

As their reward Lee and Sean had gone to have dinner with Mr. Trump's children, Donald and Ivanka. Back in the suite, Allie and I just sulked around the big empty rooms designed for eighteen people and now there were only four – soon to be three. We walked around saying goodbye to the chairs and tables and sofas. We talked about trying to convince Mr. Trump to keep both of us. Maybe if we tried hard enough, he would listen. I remember being so teary and the tears didn't come for a while, but when they did, they were just THERE. We talked about going to the boardroom and how we wouldn't be together anymore.

I went out to the balcony, looked around at everything; remembered where I was and what an opportunity I had been given. I cried, prayed, didn't know what to do. Part of me wanted to go into the boardroom and say, "Keep her. I'm cool. It's been a great ride. Sayonara." It would have been okay with me but it would be disappointing to a lot of people who helped me reach this far. I would be letting them down if I just threw in the towel. All the same I was not willing to go in there with both barrels blazing. As I tried to think about what I would say in the boardroom, I realized that the only things I could say were that we should have chosen pants instead of skirts and mention Allie's interaction with the designer. But those weren't reasons enough to fire someone. I was so sad.

Lord, I know I tried to fight you a bit, well not fight, but not give it all up to You. I held some back. Stupid, I know. But here's the thing, Lord. I'm not going to do that this time. This whole process is about the unknown, so I go in there not knowing the final outcome. I will do it with courage, knowing that you will be there.

Footprints in the Boardroom

"Prayer is simply a two-way conversation between you and God."
~Billy Graham

Roxanne Wilson

Footprints in the Boardroom

Roxanne interviews Embassy Suites' employees

Roxanne Wilson

Footprints in the Boardroom

Roxanne & Allie test the runway before the fashion show

Roxanne Wilson

Footprints in the Boardroom

The Final Four, Sean, Lee, Roxanne & Allie view the Embassy Suites fashion show

Roxanne Wilson

Chapter Fifteen

☙❧

"Pray and let God worry."
~ Martin Luther

It was a very long boardroom. Mr. Trump, Ivanka and Donald, Jr. asked Allie a lot of questions. They wanted to know what happened. They gave us a hard time about the puffy sleeves on the uniforms and asked why we designed skirts when the women had specifically asked for pants. Then they began to ask me questions. I made no effort to give any excuses, but said positive things about Allie, about her leadership, about how I thought our uniforms were attractive. Finally, after I had been so complimentary of Allie, Ivanka turned to me and said, "Roxanne, if you keep on spending time and opportunity saying positive things about Allie, we are not going to have time to listen to you when you are saying positive things about yourself."

I thought that was interesting. I realized that we weren't giving them an aggressive boardroom because that was what they were used to. Mr. Trump asked me what I should do and I said he should keep us both. He said, predictably: "That's not going to happen."

After some prodding – and it did feel like Mr. Trump and the others had cattle prods – urging us to do or say something for the camera. Eventually I said that Allie was high maintenance – which she is -- and they said that I had "attitude". Which may be, but I took offense to "attitude" because that was what Tammy had said previously. Even then I had wondered where that came from, because I felt I was able to get along with everyone.

But Allie brought it up again. Neither of the statements she nor I made were friendship-ending or life-changing. However, Mr. Trump jumped on those comments we made about each other and said we had been good friends and then we turned on each other. It was so classic. When Mr. Trump fired both of us – and we knew it was coming -- he said, "You came in as friends and are walking out as enemies." Allie said, "No, we aren't." And he said, "Yes, yes, you are," and then Mr. Trump fired us. So out in the hall, for a brief moment, I felt unsure. I turned to Allie and asked if we were still friends. Of course, we were. Still are. I do think it affected Allie more than me, because she desperately wanted to win. I didn't really want to win. I initially thought I did, but throughout the journey I realized that what I wanted more was the growth from this incredible opportunity. If I won as a result of the experience, that would be terrific, but either way I would be grateful for every moment. I just wanted to stay as long as I could.

The exchange was described as vicious, but that's not really how it was. Yes, Allie and I said some critical things. And we felt we had to defend ourselves, but that's how the boardroom is supposed to be viewed. Later while watching the broadcast, I realized that it wasn't as bad as Mr. Trump had made it out to be. Allie and I weren't disloyal to each other.

Seeing that Allie and I went in to the boardroom as friends and came out as friends; I still had to be able to answer questions about the segment because everybody had picked up on it. Nothing Allie said about me or to me, caused me to look at her and say: "Who are you? I don't know you."

People come up to me all the time and say one of three things: "You did throw Allie under the bus" – a reference to what I had said about not throwing Allie under the bus when we went to the boardroom. Or they say, "You were weak, you should have gone in for the jugular." Or, "Good for you, you stuck to your guns." It's funny to hear people's impression of what took place in that boardroom because for me, it was never that deep. I prayed. I knew that whatever I did or said I'd have to live with for the rest of my life. It might be tempting to make a stimulating five minutes on TV. But after the show is over, whatever I do is on my heart for the rest of my life. Don't get me wrong, I could ask forgiveness and it will be all gone away, but it would be forgiven, not forgotten.

Once out of the boardroom Allie and I headed for the taxi and gave our final comments and reactions to being fired. The idea is to capture the reactions of the fired candidates. Allie and I were laughing, joking, and having fun. As we drove around, it became clear that our friendship was intact, and that Allie and I would probably remain friends throughout our lives.

I had always wondered what it would feel like to be fired. I had never been fired. **Thank you, Lord.** I had heard the words from Mr. Trump's mouth, but they had never been directed at me. When I could feel it coming, I thought, "It's really not that bad." When I knew I would be going to the boardroom with the possibility of being fired, I didn't know what I would do; I didn't know if I would cry, feel disappointed or angry. But it was not the end of the world. It was not devastating. It was not life shattering. In some ways, because I got to stay so long, I might have to say, "Being fired never felt so good."

It's funny because my intentions in the beginning were to win. And I qualified that in a way, because I wanted to be there the entire time. I wanted to experience as much as I could. I wanted to win and I wanted to be the last woman standing. It's interesting, because when you pray for something, you may not know how God is going to answer your prayer. He may not answer the way in which you think you want him to, but I believe he answers. I prayed that I wouldn't be the first fired – and I wasn't. And I was one of the last two women standing. I don't think you have to be too specific. Give God a little bit of wiggle room – not that He needs wiggle room. Maybe God was saying to me, "You weren't meant to be *The Apprentice*, so you aren't, but you were to get a glimpse of what is possible." Maybe it was just a stop, a rest stop on the journey I'm supposed to be on.

The whole concept of winning is interesting, because in reality, everybody won just by participating in the process. Summer was the first one fired, but she won – because she beat out all those hundreds of thousands of applicants to reach to that point. She stood up for what she believed and left with dignity. I think that is winning.

Lord, once again I thank you for the opportunity to have come this far. I am so happy and feel so fortunate for all I have experienced and am ready to start the next journey you have in store for me. No resistance Lord, courage, confidence and bravery. Amen.

> "Evening and at morning, and at noon, I will pray and cry aloud; and He shall hear my voice."
> ~Psalms 55:17

Footprints in the Boardroom

Roxanne & Allie in their final boardroom

Roxanne Wilson

Chapter Sixteen

❦

"Praying without ceasing is not ritualized, nor are there even words. It is a constant state of awareness of oneness with God."
~Peace Pilgrim

God, seriously, I have always believed I have a purpose, and as I get older I am less and less clear what that purpose is, but I look to You and pray for answers.

After riding around for some time talking about our adventure in the board room, Allie and I went back to the suite. Because the search for Mr. Trump's apprentice was down to the last task with Lee and Sean, all the previous applicants traveled back for the finale. That night Lee and Sean were to choose their teammates to help on the final task.

Seeing everyone again was weird. At the same time it was so cool because the others had gone on with their lives and we had been living in this bubble. After each candidate was fired, we said goodbye and got busy with the next task, but we didn't really forget them. It was somewhat strange seeing Tammy. There was a little time to talk to her and tell her how hurt I was, and that I thought we were friends. She responded rather vaguely, saying only that I was thinking about myself, not her. Because I knew that not only had I been thinking about her, but had prayed for her as well, I felt her statement was rather ironic; however, I didn't want to say, "Oh yes I was, and I even prayed for you." So I just left it alone.

Later we were able to talk more about it and it became "water under the bridge." That was a relief because I did not want any strife between Tammy and me. I realize that in a pressure cooker situation like *The Apprentice* those who stay through the end are working on no sleep and lots of stress. Things happen between good people that are hurtful but remembering who I am and who Tammy is at our core, enabled me to move forward. The experience with Tammy and soon after that, being fired put it all in perspective and gave me more fire for the last task. My wounds were still open and raw but I felt like I had something to prove. On the other hand, I find it so stimulating to be totally present to experience everything, even the bad times. I wanted to taste the good and the bad. But when I tasted the bad, I didn't like it so much. You hope that all the bad things that happen don't affect you to the core, because you do have a strong foundation. You can shake it off because you are a child of God and it's all going to be all right. I remember that in my darkest moments at times I felt like I was suffocating in negativity. But I was able to bounce back.

Lord, as much as I was hurt by the betrayal, I am conscious of the need of support and comfort of those who hurt me. Lord, you have been wonderful to me in the past and I pray that you will continue to bestow blessings on me.

Footprints in the Boardroom

Give me courage, for I fear nothing with You as my guide and my salvation.

I was excited Lee chose me to be on his team. It was huge! I had never worked with Lee, but he was impressed because I was the only project manager to beat him and I managed to beat him handily on the Rutgers task. To know that he recognized and appreciated my value and wanted me on his team was a compliment.

It was especially rewarding to work with Lys, the executive director of the Leary Firefighters Foundation. She asked us lots of questions, eliciting our ideas and often said, "Listen to Roxanne. She knows what she is doing." And I did. I knew how to run an auction. For two years I had run the major auction at the University of Michigan Law School- I could produce a successful silent auction as well as a live auction- so that was a profound affirmation of my work. There were other times when she would be looking for me and say: "Where is Roxanne? I need to talk to her." To know that Lee as well as the executives recognized my abilities made me feel so much better seeing that I had spent so much time the previous days doubting my skills.

There are times in the process of carrying out a project that we do question our abilities. I remember doing that in law school I wrote in my prayer journal.

I need to accept the fact that I am smart and stop defeating myself internally. My biggest barrier is me. My lack of self-confidence. I need to accept where I have been and believe that I am qualified to be where I am now.

Working for Lee also gave me the opportunity to be a servant. Robert Greenleaf, founder of the Greenleaf Center for Servant Leadership defined servant leadership as: "It begins with the natural feeling that one wants to serve. Then conscious choice brings one to aspire to lead." I've thought about this a lot. In college, I remember a quote from Albert Schweitzer that went something like "the only people who find true happiness are those who serve." For me, I think it is Biblical. In Chamber, a service organization at Baylor University, we had a saying, "A Chamber man paints the back of the fence." Doing all you can but not requiring, requesting, or expecting accolades for it. That was what I tried to do while on Lee's team. I was there to work for him, help him, and do all that I could to see that he was successful.

I saw other examples of servant leadership throughout the show. On both of my tasks as project manager, Allie worked her tail off to assist me. During the Norwegian Cruise Line task, Allie not only supported me when no one else did, but she worked hard through her illness to make sure that we got quality shots. During the Rutgers task, Allie took the lead on procuring deals with the cheerleading squad and sold the Outback Steakhouse food like a champion.

Leadership is more than taking control. It is listening to your teammates and anticipating the needs of the whole group. Leaders attempt to persuade their followers, not dictate to them.

Another event which started out as serving and progressed into leading was creating the jingle for the Arby's task. As I've already said, writing a jingle is right down my alley. My teammates repeatedly expressed how impressed they were at how I was able to start running with the jingle concept. When the time came to go to the studio and lay down the track, Sean - the project manager on the task- took me into the studio and gave me creative lead to choose the instruments, beat and style of the jingle. The experience was so rewarding for me because it provided an opportunity to share my gifts and talents. I was so energized that suddenly I was leading the team through the process. It was never my intention to emerge into the leadership role, but I am so glad that I did. Not only did I learn more about servant leadership, but I also regained confidence in my own abilities.

While working with Lee on the last task was challenging, the other thing that seemed so strange was competing against three of my former teammates – Sean, Tammy and Andrea -- the three with whom I had the most conflict. And they took the name "Synergy", while Lee kept "Gold Rush." Now I was working for Lee and Gold Rush. There wasn't much time to think about what that felt like – to be working against my former teammates. But as the

Footprints in the Boardroom

fifth season of *The Apprentice* neared its end, I did realize that I was still learning so much from the entire experience.

When the process was all over, I had learned from the curve ball I was thrown by Tammy and I was able to bounce back. God was able to show me, "You do have your doubts" and I do have my doubts, uncertainties about things from time to time, but He always washes my doubts away. Some might think that I would still have reservations because Lee's team lost and Sean was hired as Mr. Trump's apprentice. But in reality I had met many of my goals. I stayed until the last task; I was one of the last two women standing; I was totally present in every experience; I had emerged with a renewed confidence in my worthiness.

Stepping out on the balcony for the last time, I looked around at the city and thought about what a remarkable few months this had been. The Abercrombie and Fitch store that had been draped while under construction was now complete. I smiled as I heard the familiar sound of the saxophone trickle over to the balcony one last time. The skyline peeked through the skyscrapers as I watched the people walk home from their jobs. I remembered the parade that had passed through the streets one morning with all of the celebration. I knew I would miss this city and all the life that pulses through the streets. I had conquered the big city and now I felt new life breathe through me.

Dear Lord I have no complaints or regrets. What a blessing that is. I told myself when I first came to New York that I must make goals, but first and last it is all Your will. I am so fortunate. Thank you, Lord.

※

> "You pray in your distress and your need; would that you would pray also in the fullness of your joy and in your days of abundance."
> ~Kahlil Gibran

Roxanne Wilson

Footprints in the Boardroom

***Lee presents his final team:
Lee, Lenny, Roxanne, & Pepi***

Roxanne Wilson

Chapter Seventeen

☙❧

"I have been driven many times to my knees by the overwhelming conviction that I had nowhere else to go."
~Abraham Lincoln

I've been asked if I experienced loneliness during my stint with *The Apprentice*. Yes, there were times when I was lonely, feeling completely alone, but I didn't get homesick. I've never understood why kids get homesick. I was always the girl who went to choir camp for two weeks and tried not to forget to call home. I just didn't get homesick. I was having a wonderful adventure and it was like, wow, what an opportunity! Sure, I missed my family and friends, but I knew they were there, so I just enjoyed the adventure.

Roxanne Wilson

> *Lord, I pray that you will continue to take me further in this journey...This process is becoming more and more complicated and I need to keep my head on. I need to stay focused and true to who I am. This is my goal – to maintain who I am. To "be Roxanne." If I lose being me, then I lose everything. Help me to be focused and to trust and rely on you.*

Loneliness seemed to arise when I was fearful, or when I took a stand that was against the majority. When I stood up for Brent after our first loss, I felt very alone in that boardroom. Again, after the Rutgers task. Allie, Tammy and I had been so together, but I knew if we did not win then, as project manager, I would have to go. This would be through no fault or limitation of anyone, but it was a very lonely feeling. However, it was the reality of how the game was played.

Loneliness arose again when I was selected to return for the final task. Lee chose me to be on the Gold Rush team as he and Sean battled for the job as Mr. Trump's apprentice. As excited as I was to return for the final task, I was embarking into new territory. I had never worked with Lee before, but I was confident that he asked me because he felt I could help him win. I had never worked with Lenny before, either, and only with Pepi on two tasks before he was fired. I was working against three of my former teammates. It was weird. Everything I knew, everything I was comfortable with was gone. All I wanted was do a good job for Lee, but I felt very alone on that task.

The times I felt the most alone were when I was trying to do everything on my own instead of relying on God. Praying was my salvation. Prayer and hand-written notes like this one from my sister renewed my spirits:

Footprints in the Boardroom

> " *Foxy, Roxy,*
> *We hope all is well! All the stuff in this box will hopefully work. The toe warmers can be placed in your pockets... Hang in there, champ. Remember... no matter what happens we still ♥ you and are very proud. I am sure you showed them what it means to be a "Wilson"! Take care! We ♥ you!! Be safe!!*
> *-Love, Rochelle, Jeffrey & Bear.*"

On the note were little sayings like "*way to go*" and "*nice hair*".

I knew that no matter what happened, I was not alone. I *did* have my family and friends backing me; and God was by my side. So when I went into the boardroom or dealt with any other adversity, I knew who I was and what I had to do.

Life is hard and oh so challenging. But Lord, I thank you for the gift of always knowing even in my loneliest hour that you are there and that the "staples" you have put in my life are there for me, too. A staple holds important things together. Lord, I thank you for the staples in life that I sometimes take for granted. I thank you for my family and friends who know me good and bad, and yet call me daughter, sister, and friend. As I travel through life and face challenges I thank you for the "staples" whose support holds me together and reminds me that I am not alone and I can face anything. Amen.

☙❧

"*A generous prayer is never presented in vain; the petition may be refused, but the petitioner is always, I believe, rewarded by some gracious visitation.*"
~Robert Louis Stevenson

133

Roxanne Wilson

Footprints in the Boardroom

Chapter Eighteen

☙❧

"There is not in the world a kind of life more sweet and delightful than that of a continual conversation with God."
~Brother Lawrence

When I was young and for years afterward I said my prayers beginning with: "Now I lay me down to sleep, I pray the Lord my soul to keep. If I should die before I wake, I pray the Lord my soul to take." Even as a teenager and a young adult, I ritually started my prayers with that childhood prayer. Then I would go on to my bedtime prayers. There is comfort in saying prayers in a familiar way. Comfort in knowing you are on a personal basis with God, like the friend in the room.

There is no doubt that God was with me through the entire process of being on *The Apprentice*. He was present in the dark times and in the bright times, in the suite, on the balcony and in the boardroom. But now I have a more informal relationship with God. I approach him in a more casual way, "Hey, God, how are you doin'?" I even joke with him and I guess it is okay, because he hasn't struck me with a lightening bolt or anything. That is how I feel. God is with me at all times.

When I returned home after participating in *The Apprentice*, nothing was the same.

Before I left Austin to be on *The Apprentice*, I had my routine: teach Jazzercise at 6 .a.m. – which I loved, go to work – at Winstead, a job I loved, do my Komen activities, hang out with friends, participate in church activities, then start the day over again. I was always active, but doing the same things over and over again. After returning to Austin, I just could not pick up where I had left off. I felt different. Several of my friends even said I was different. But I think some saw me as a character, the girl on television, in the magazine, or in the newspaper article.

Certainly I was different. Oh, I was the same Roxanne, but I had traveled in Mr. Trump's jet, on his helicopter, lived in a palatial suite, got a diamond, sung with Burt Bacharach, and taken a jet to DC to meet with Senator Schumer. I got a glimpse of what it was like to do projects for Fortune 100 companies. Those things were awesome, but they didn't make me different in the sense that I felt better than anyone else. What made me different were the things I learned about myself. It was rather like going to a foreign country. You almost always have your horizons broadened and your world view expanded when you travel abroad. That is how I was different. Gaining knowledge of what I could do, and probably what I should do with the gifts that God has given me created in me a desire to strive for the next peak.

It's almost as if God re-charged my battery and the most ungrateful thing I could have done would be to say, "Thanks for the charge, God," and simply go back to the same things I was doing, without evaluating what next I should do with my life.

Just recently at a conference in Los Angeles, I asked a man sitting next to me if the business strategies we were learning about really worked, or was it just a scam. He said emphatically, "Yes, they work IF people go back to their lives and put the practices into action." He said there were a lot of participants who are conference junkies, who attend conferences and workshops, spend thousands of dollars, then go back to their job and not change a thing. They never apply what they have learned.

Being on *The Apprentice* was life-changing for me. And when we have those life-changing moments we have to implement the change. God gives the spark; we have to start the fire. If we don't, then it's wasted. What do we do with that life-changing moment? It's quite possible that you can have life-changing experiences that say: "Your life is exactly where it ought to be." Because that can happen, too.

It was also life-changing in that I had to rely on what I thought was the right thing to do without worrying about parents, sisters, friends, and even Baylor University. At first I said to myself, "Roxanne, you went to a Christian school and you have a responsibility to not cause great destruction or shame to the school." So that was weighing on me. First of all, I'm not so important that I could bring disgrace on Baylor, and regardless I knew I would never compromise my beliefs and my morals. What I did have to do was put myself out there to experience all I could and just focus on what I felt was right in my heart. Forget what my parents and friends would think. I had to put my faith in God and not my second grade teacher or my pastor. Still there were things I wasn't willing to do. I wasn't willing to walk into the boardroom and ask Mr. Trump to fire Brent when he didn't do anything to cause the team's loss. I wasn't willing to hide my feelings for people and situations just to go farther in the competition.

Returning to reality was interesting in the way that different groups reacted to me. My Jazzercise students were wonderful. They saw the show and enjoyed it thoroughly, but they treated me the same.

My family? They were fantastic! Each one had a different take on what they were curious about. My dad is more bottom line, wanting to know specifics about where, when and how things happened. My mom, Patricia, wants the flowery stuff: Who did you meet? What were they like? My older sister was a mix of Dad and Mom. Wanting specifics, but what people looked like, how did they behave? And my youngest sister wanted to know who was with whom, what they wore, what kind of nail polish they wore, how their hair looked. They are great. They were totally supportive the whole time I was on *The Apprentice*. My dad is very traditional and watched with a serious concentration. My mom is more conservative and would get upset when I was bleeped. "Oh Roxanne!" she would say. My sisters told me how she reacted to those times.

My experience has actually brought my family closer together. And that is just another positive spin-off of the adventure. They are still as solid and as stable as ever and they are my home base. I travel a lot now and it's nice to have people come up to me and say "I know you. You were on TV." I like it. But it's also nice to go home and just be me. I like to hang out with my nephew, just relax, and be in a comforting cocoon. My younger sister, when asked what it was like to see me on TV, said "People see Roxanne on TV and think they know her. *They* don't know her. I know her. **I** know Roxanne."

Returning to my church gave me another perspective on how my life had changed. I had said to one of my friends in the young professionals group, *Untitled*, that when I came back, I didn't want to know anybody. By that I meant that I hoped the group would have grown with so many new people that I wouldn't recognize them. When that really happened I was surprised. Surprised, but pleased. I was glad that it was successful, that what we had started the year before had grown and flourished. It had been such a wonderful experience to start the organization. But I believe that everything you do prepares you for something in the future, and God may have pulled me away to do something different. There were so many capable people continuing *Untitled's* success, it was encouraging to see how they had grown.

The number one question I am asked about my experience is what Mr. Trump is actually like. All of my impressions, memories, and experiences with Mr. Trump are positive. In addition to being smart, Mr. Trump has the three "C's": courage, confidence and charisma. What sets Mr. Trump apart from others is the last "C" – his immense charisma. It gives him the ability to be blunt, forthright, and honest, and still be heard. I admire all that he has accomplished and all he will accomplish, and I feel fortunate that he gave me the opportunity to experience such an intense job interview process – *The Apprentice.*

Someone said the three most important questions in life were: Who are you? Where are you going? And who will go with you? That's kind of like asking the question: What is the meaning of life?

I am a child of God. I am going wherever God leads me. My family, my friends, my faith community and My God will go with me. I'm this big ball of mass who is trying to get to the end goal-- wherever that might be-- who honors God and is true to my sense of what honoring God means. I think it is different for everybody. I'm just like a lot of people trying to make the world better. Now I sound like I'm running for Miss Universe. *"Yes, I'm a child of God who wants world peace."* But I do think my faith makes me who I am, what causes me to do and not do a lot of things. Right now, knowing where I came from and where I am now is enough.

When I was four years old, I said I wanted to be a Supreme Court Justice. I carved out a path, a difficult path, because I just can't sit around and wait for life to just happen for me. So I did well in school, college, went to Law School, clerked for the Texas Supreme Court, worked at a prestigious law firm in Austin. And I come to this juncture in my life with eyes wide open and eager for the next step.

I do feel if I keep going forward step after step, then the path will be made clearer. I find comfort in that. I do want to know what I will be doing with my life and I'm moving forward with faith.

Through my journey I have learned ten keys to being successful. These ten keys are:

1. With great risk comes great success,
2. Leadership lies within those who are willing to serve,
3. To be successful you must have a strong foundation,
4. There is more to life than business – Balance is Key,
5. The best work is done when you are internally motivated,
6. The right answer is often the hard answer,
7. There is a place for friendship in business,

8. Always have a backup plan/ exit strategy/ rainy day schedule,
9. Don't forget those who helped you along the way,
10. Don't take yourself too seriously.

I know that wherever I go, as long as I remember those ten things, I will be the best Roxanne I can be.

Eventually, I want to find the right mate, get married, have kids, all that. I want stability, flexibility, time to spend with family, be involved in my community – the church community, the larger community, organizations like Komen and Make a Wish Foundation. What is important to me is being able to spend time with those I love and helping them as well as others. Who will go with me? My family, my friends - the whole world. Everyone's invited on the Roxanne train. Everybody!

I truly believe that God has a plan for me. I just need to voice my desires. I think words are so powerful. You never know which thoughts are going to come into fruition and which will not. Probably the ones that are God-led are the ones that will spring to life. The key is to take every step with the faith and knowledge that God is always there, always leading. In the moments where the next step is uncertain, take solace in the fact that you are never alone, that oftentimes in your darkest moments He has been carrying you.

I'm exploring new territory. I'm learning as I go, trying new things, networking. Bless my Dad's heart; he's an educator and for him the process is: you get the book, you take the courses, you follow the instructions - my method is a little stressful for him. But this it so invigorating because there is no set, defined way to go about it. You can reach your goals in so many different ways, so many adventurous paths, just have faith.

It's exciting. It's mysterious. I never know what phone call or email I'm going to get or where I'm going next or who I'm going to meet. I like it. I love it! And I think God every day!

Footprints in the Boardroom

Now I lay me down to sleep, I pray the lord my soul to keep. Hey God, it's me Roxanne. Thank you, thank you, thank you. Amen

☙❧

Roxanne in the Trump boardroom

Roxanne Wilson

Quotation Sources

❧

Introduction
"Every wish is like a prayer – with God."
Source: Elizabeth Barrett Browning - giga-usa.com

"Prayer is the key of the morning and the bolt of the evening."
Source: Mohandas Gandhi - brainyquote.com

❧

Chapter 1
"Prayer does not change God, but it changes him who prays."
Source: Soren Kierkegaard - quotegarden.com

Chapter 2
"Prayer is the confession of one's unworthiness and weakness."
Source: Mohandas Gandhi - brainyquote.com
"Do not be anxious about anything, but in everything, by prayer and petition, with thanksgiving, present your requests to God. And the peace of God, which transcends all understanding, will guard your hearts and your minds in Christ Jesus."
Source: Philippians 4:6-7 (NRSV)

Chapter 3
"If the only prayer you ever say in your whole life is 'thank you' that would suffice."
Source: Meister Eckhart - quotationspage.com

"Faith and prayer are the vitamins of the soul: man cannot live in health without them."
Source: Mahalia Jackson - brainyquote.com

Chapter 4
"Prayer is nothing else than being on terms of friendship with God."
Source: Saint Teresa - brainyquote.com

"Do not pray for easy lives. Pray to be stronger men. Do not pray for a task equal to your powers, pray for powers equal to your task."
Source: Phillips Brooks - quotationspage.com

Chapter 5
"Prayer does not use up artificial energy, doesn't burn up any fossil fuel, doesn't pollute. Neither does song, neither does love, neither does the dance."
Source: Margaret Mead - brainyquote.com

"Pray for a tough hide and a tender heart."
Source: Ruth Graham - quotegarden.com

Chapter 6
"Certain thoughts are prayers. There are moments when, whatever be the attitude of the body, the soul is on the knees."
Source: Victor Hugo - brainyquote.com

"When we take one step toward God, he takes seven steps toward us."
Source: Indian Proverb - entwagon.com

Chapter 7
"Don't pray when it rains if you don't pray when the sun shines."
Source: Satchel Paige. - quotegarden.com
"God can pick sense out of a confused prayer."
Source: Richard Sibbes - quotegarden.com

Chapter 8
"Pray as if everything depended on God and work as if everything depended upon man."
Source: Francis Cardinal Spellman - quotationspage.com

"A simple grateful thought turned heavenwards is the most perfect prayer."
Source: G. E. Lessing - quotationspage.com

❧❦

Chapter 9
"Is any among you suffering? Let him pray. Is any cheerful? Let him sing praise."
Source: James 5:13

"As we express our gratitude, we must never forget that the highest appreciation is not to utter words, but to live by them."
Source: John Fitzgerald Kennedy - tentmaker.org

Chapter 10
"Prayer begins where human capacity ends. "
Source: Marian Anderson - giga-usa.com

"God speaks in the silence of the heart. Listening is the beginning of prayer."
Source: Mother Teresa - quotegarden.com

❧❦

Chapter 11
"Our prayers should be for blessings in general, for God knows best what is good for us."
Source: Socrates - entwagon.com

"But when you pray, go into your room, close the door and pray to your Father, who is unseen. Then your Father, who sees what is done in secret, will reward you."
Source: Matthew 6:6

❧❦

Chapter 12
"Call on God, but row away from the rocks."
Source: Indian Proverb - quotegarden.com

"Arranging a bowl of flowers in the morning can give a sense of quiet in a crowded day – like writing a poem or saying a prayer."
Source: Anne Morrow Lindbergh - quotationspage.com

Chapter 13
"Pray that you will never have to bear all that you are able to endure."
Source: Jewish Proverb - entwagon.com
"Grace isn't a little prayer you chant before receiving a meal. It's a way to live."
Source: Jackie Windspear - tentmaker.org

Chapter 14
"Our prayers should be for blessings in general, because God knows best what is good for us."
Source: Socrates - entwagon.com

"Prayer is simply a two-way conversation between you and God."
Source: Billy Graham - lifeway.com

Chapter 15
"Pray and let God worry."
Source: Martin Luther - tentmaker.org

"Evening, morning, and noon, I cry out in distress, and He hears my voice."
Source: Psalms 55:17

Chapter 16

"Praying without ceasing is not ritualized, nor are there even words. It is a constant state of awareness of oneness with God."
Source: Peace Pilgrim - thinkexist.com

"You pray in your distress and your need; would that you would pray also in the fullness of your joy and in your days of abundance."
Source: Kahlil Gibran - brainyquote.com

Chapter 17

"I have been driven many times to my knees by the overwhelming conviction that I had nowhere else to go." Abraham Lincoln - quotegarden.com

"A generous prayer is never presented in vain; the petition may be refused, but the petitioner is always, I believe, rewarded by some gracious visitation."
Source: Robert Louis Stevenson - yuni.com

Chapter 18

"There is not in the world a kind of life more sweet and delightful than that of a continual conversation with God."
Source: Brother Lawrence - tentmaker.org

Biography

֍

Roxanne Wilson, an appellate attorney and President and CEO of RXW, Inc., recently completed season five of Donald Trump's "The Apprentice"; gaining rave reviews from "The Donald" himself. Roxanne was the first African-American woman to compete in the final four on the NBC hit show. She is the President & CEO of RXW, incorporated, a Texas based consulting firm. Prior, she worked as an appellate attorney with Winstead Sechrest & Minick P.C. law firm in Austin, Texas. Roxanne also clerked for two justices of the Texas Supreme Court. Roxanne earned her law degree at the University of Michigan where she was awarded the Irving Stenn Jr. award for her contributions to the University of Michigan Law School.

Roxanne Wilson

Outside of her law career, Roxanne dedicates her time and talents to support causes and organizations close to her heart. Roxanne is currently the spokesperson for the Make A Wish Foundation Destination Joy presented by Lay's. Roxanne also serves on the Susan G. Komen Breast Cancer Foundation Austin Affiliate Board of Directors and is a provisional member of the Junior League of Austin.

Roxanne received a BBA in Economics at Baylor University in Texas. While at Baylor, Roxanne became the first woman and second African American member of the prestigious Baylor Chamber of Commerce - for which she later served as President. Roxanne continues to serve Baylor as a Baylor Alumni Association Board member, Student Life Advisory Board member, Baylor Business Network Austin committee member, Baylor Young Grad Network Austin committee member, and avid supporter of Baylor sports.

Roxanne is a national public speaker who is sought after by women's organizations, Christian groups, colleges, universities, and young professional organizations. Her lectures are inspiring as she challenges you to reach for the star within. Roxanne is also the new co-host of *Inspire the Desire*; Texas' own Christian Talent Search television program.

Roxanne is committed to maintaining a sound mind, body and spirit. She grew up in the church and served as the assistant director of children's musicals and sang in the choir. Seeing the need for a young professionals group at Riverbend Church, Roxanne and several others founded *Untitled*.

As a certified Jazzercise Instructor, Roxanne is in top physical shape. Roxanne successfully trained and auditioned to become an independent Jazzercise franchisee, enabling her to enhance the lives of others through exercise and dance. Born in Ames, Iowa, Roxanne is the middle child in a trio of sisters. Her family moved to Arizona when Roxanne was six years old. Roxanne approaches every opportunity and challenge with curiosity and enthusiasm.

Footprints in the Boardroom

Kathryn Miller is a former teacher, school social worker and school counselor. Since retirement, she works as editor for educational publications and writes inspirational essays on women's issues. Kathryn lives in Austin, Texas with her husband.

Roxanne Wilson